Foundations for the faith

Foundations for the faith

A step-by-step study guide to the Gospel of John

Roger Ellsworth

PUBLISHING WITH A MISSION

EP BOOKS
Faverdale North, Darlington, DL3 0PH, England

e-mail: sales@epbooks.org

EP BOOKS USA
P. O. Box 614, Carlisle, PA 17013, USA

e-mail: usa.sales@epbooks.org

web: http://www.epbooks.org

First published 2009

British Library Cataloguing in Publication Data available

ISBN-13 978-0-85234-615-0   ISBN 0-85234-615-8

Printed and bound in Great Britain by MPG Biddles Ltd, King's Lynn, Norfolk.

To my dear friends,
Jeff, Lori, Aaron, Nathan and Rebekah Holt

Contents

Preface and acknowledgements

I assured myself many years ago that I would never write a book on John's Gospel. The ground has been traversed so often by so many who are so much more capable than I. What would be the point?

But here I am offering this volume! My reasons for doing so are twofold. Firstly, even old truth needs new packaging from time to time. Secondly, while I pretend to offer no startling insights in these comments, the 'packaging' will, I trust, contribute much to making this study worthwhile. This packaging consists of a memory verse at the beginning of each chapter, my outline and comments with quotes from others interspersed throughout and 'Digging Deeper' and 'Action' sections at the end.

Students who master the memory verses will carry away from this study fifty-two verses that will encourage and strengthen them.

The quotes from others will not only contribute to understanding the passage at hand but will also encourage the students to read some of these works for themselves.

The 'Digging Deeper' and 'Action' sections are intended to drive the student more deeply into the Scripture which is indeed a lamp to our feet and a light to our path (Ps. 119:105).

It is all arranged in fifty-two chapters — ideal for a weekly study group to cover the entire Gospel in one year.

As always, I am indebted to many: David Clark, formerly of Evangelical Press, for planting this idea with me; my wife Sylvia for capably assisting me in many ways; and my Pastor's Class for gladly receiving these chapters in lecture form.

Most of all, I am profoundly grateful to the Holy Spirit of God for inspiring the apostle to write this exhilarating portrayal of 'The Lamb of God who takes away the sin of the world' (John 1:29). My study of it has often caused me to be 'lost in wonder, love and praise'.

Roger Ellsworth
September 2009

Introduction

The Gospel of John may very well be the best loved of all the books of the Bible. The early Christians used the eagle to symbolize this Gospel, and most of us readily agree it is a fitting symbol because the Gospel indeed causes our minds and hearts to soar.

There used to be some debate over the author of the book, but it is now virtually undisputed that the man whose name it bears was its author. This is, of course, John, the son of Zebedee, and one of Jesus' inner circle of disciples.

The date of his writing was probably around A.D. 90, and his readers were probably Christians in Ephesus. His purpose is clearly stated in 20:30-31, namely, that his readers 'may believe that Jesus is the Christ, the Son of God'.

John was undoubtedly concerned to convince any unbelievers who might happen to read his Gospel that they were in need of Christ, but his original readers were already believers. Why would John, then, write that they may believe? The force of the word 'believe' in 20:31 is 'that you may go on believing'.

It is not hard to see why John found it necessary to urge his readers in this way. It had been almost sixty years since Jesus had been crucified, had risen from the dead and had ascended to the Father. Many false teachers had arisen to challenge the basic facts of the gospel, advancing a whole set of beliefs that essentially destroyed the Christian faith. Some were asserting that Jesus was not equal to God before he came to this world. They further alleged that he certainly was not God after he came. Known as 'Gnostics' (from the Greek word *'gnosis'* — to know), these teachers stated that their views had come to them through special enlightenment from God himself.

By the time John wrote his Gospel, all the other apostles had died. These were the men to whom believers had looked for strength and guidance, men who had fanned the flames of faith and had battled fiercely against the false teachers. Now they were gone, and the teachings of the heretics began to take on the hue of plausibility. I can see the aged John sadly surveying the situation and exclaiming to himself: 'If only these young Christians could see what I saw and hear what I heard. They wouldn't be swayed by these false teachers.'

His readers could not, of course, see what he had seen and hear what he had heard, but they could do the next best thing, namely, read John's account of what had occurred. So John picked up his pen and, under the inspiration of the Holy Spirit, produced this grand and glorious Gospel.

But how could he, John, best secure his purpose? How could he encourage believers who were in danger of drifting to hold to the truth about Jesus? A survey of his Gospel shows his strategy.

- He begins with the thunderous affirmation that Jesus was fully God both before and after he came to this earth.

- He proceeds to show that Jesus demonstrated his deity through the miracles that he performed. Out of the vast number of such miracles (20:30; 21:25), John selects seven that unquestionably proved the nature of Jesus.

Introduction

- He also presents major discourses (5:19-47; 6:32-58; 10:1-38; 14:1 - 16:33) in which Jesus clearly claimed to be nothing less than God. The 'I am' sayings of Jesus, most of which are found in the discourses (6:35; 8:12; 10:7,11; 11:25; 14:6; 15:1), served as pointed reminders to the Jews that God had identified himself as 'I AM WHO I AM' (Exod. 3:14). While Jesus' statement, 'Before Abraham was, I AM,' is not usually counted among the 'I am' statements mentioned above, it serves as the most clear-cut connection with God's affirmation in Exodus 3:14.

- John also presents the witness of God the Father to the divine identity of Jesus. This witness made use of John the Baptist (1:19-34; 5:33-35), the works or miracles mentioned above (5:36; 10:25,32,38; 14:10-11) and Scripture (5:39). In addition to these, John records an occasion in which the Father spoke from heaven to confirm Jesus as his Son (12:28).

- In addition to showing how the Father witnessed to Jesus, the apostle also declares that Jesus revealed the Father (1:14,18; 14:9-11). The point is quite simple — for Jesus to reveal God as he did, he had to be God.

- The apostle John further shows his readers that the very Holy Spirit they had professed to receive had come for the express purpose of revealing the truth about Jesus (14:15-18; 15:26-27; 16:5-15).

- John points to both the crucifixion and resurrection of Jesus as insurmountable proofs of his deity. The former, which some regarded as evidence that Jesus was not God, actually proved that he was. It was the 'hour' for which he had come to this world (2:4; 7:6,8,30; 8:20; 12:23,27-

13

28; 13:1; 17:1). Furthermore, it fulfilled the prophecies of the Old Testament (19:24,36-37) and finished the mission assigned to him by the Father (19:30). The resurrection, which itself was substantiated by the empty tomb, the peculiar configuration of the cloths in which Jesus' body had been wrapped and his appearances to his disciples leave no doubt that Jesus was God in human flesh.

The whole Gospel constitutes, then, an impressive and convincing argument regarding the identity of Jesus. It is surely not coincidence that caused John to share Thomas' words to Jesus, 'My Lord and my God!' (20:28), immediately before stating the purpose of his Gospel (20:30-31).

Thomas' words are a fitting culmination to the thread of testimony that runs throughout the Gospel: from John the Baptist (1:34), Nathaniel (1:49), Simon Peter (6:69) and Martha (11:27).

As we work our way through the evidence amassed by John in this Gospel, we can at the end, with the help of the Spirit of God, do no other than take our place alongside Thomas and the others and take their words as our own.

'John "gives us more of the mystery" while Matthew, Mark and Luke give us "the history"'

(Matthew Henry,
Matthew Henry's Commentary, vol. v, p.847).

First Quarter

The deity of Jesus

'And the Word became flesh and dwelt among us, and we beheld his glory, the glory as of the only begotten of the Father, full of grace and truth' (1:14).

John's opening verses show us that he had no time for preliminaries; the issue was too great for that. So he plunged right into the very heart of the matter. False teachers, known as Gnostics, were championing a whole cluster of beliefs that essentially destroyed the Christian message. Some denied that Jesus was equal to God before he came into this world, even maintaining that he was the least in a whole series of gods under the true God. Another common belief was that Jesus was not really God when he was born in Bethlehem.

In his first eighteen verses, known as the Prologue, John answers these assertions by showing that Jesus was God both before and after he came to this earth.

Jesus was God before his coming (vv. 1-5)

John challenged the assumption that Jesus was not God in human flesh by calling him 'the Word'. We reveal what is on our minds through words. So words involve both comprehension and the communication of our thoughts. By calling Jesus 'the Word', John was saying that Jesus perfectly comprehends God and reveals him to us.

'[Jesus as the Word] … has made known God's mind to us, as a man's word or speech makes known his thoughts, as far as he pleases and no further… He is *the Word* speaking *from* God to us, and *to God* for us' (italics are his).

(Matthew Henry,
Commentary on the Whole Bible, vol. v, p.848).

Jesus was God after his coming (vv. 6-18)

John the Baptist testified to it (vv. 6-8,15)

'The Old Testament prophets cried aloud, to show people their sins; this New Testament prophet cried aloud, to show people their Saviour'

(Matthew Henry, vol. v, p.855).

Individual enlightenment testifies to it (vv. 9-13)

Every person who comes into this world is enlightened in some ways. He sees the creation of God, he has the ability to reason, and he has a conscience. All of these things are given to him by Christ. Further light is given to many of us through the preaching of the gospel.

The great wretchedness of men and women lies at this very point. Even though the light of God has shone brightly throughout history, they cannot see it. The light of God never shined more brightly than when the Lord Jesus came to this world. He came to his own people, people who had been given the promise of his coming and had every reason to accept him as the Messiah; but they rejected him (vv. 10-11). If people cannot see the light shining at its brightest, the fault is not with the light, but with the people themselves. A blind person cannot see light no matter how brightly it shines, and all of us are by nature blinded by sin.

How, then, is anyone saved? It is certainly not due to anything a person himself does to cast off his blindness, but rather to the gracious work of God in his heart (vv. 12-13).

The apostles testified to it (v. 14)

1. *What they saw.* On one hand they saw flesh because Jesus was a real human being, but it was obvious that he was no ordinary man because they could also see in him the glory of God.

'The greatest honour that ever was put upon this world, which is so mean and inconsiderable a part of the universe, was that the Son of God was once *in the world...*'
(Matthew Henry, vol. v, p.851, italics are his).

2. *What they concluded.* He was the only begotten of the Father full of grace and truth.

All believers can testify to it (vv. 16-17)

We have noted that the believer is saved by the grace of God. Yet the grace we receive in salvation is merely the first instalment. From the moment he is saved the believer receives grace on top of grace. All the believer's experiences of God's grace are proof that Jesus was indeed God in human flesh.

John's conclusion from the facts he has presented in verses 1-17 is clear. The human Jesus perfectly reveals the God no one has ever seen (v. 18). How could Jesus do this if he were not the person he claimed to be, namely, God in human flesh?

DIGGING   DEEPER

1. *Read John 1:1-5. What five assertions does the apostle make about Jesus?*

2. *Read verses 6-8. What features of the ministry of John the Baptist can you identify?*

3. *Read verse 9. In what ways does the Lord Jesus Christ give light 'to every man'?*

4. *Read verses 10-13. These verses mention a 'right' and a birth. What is the right? How does the birth take place?*

5. *Read verse 14. What did the disciples of Jesus see as they 'beheld' him?*

6. *Read verse 15. What did John the Baptist mean by saying Jesus was 'preferred' before him?*

7. *Read verses 16-18. What do you think the apostle John means with the words 'grace for grace'? If grace refers to the mercy of God, and truth refers to the justice of God, how did Jesus blend 'grace and truth'?*

 The apostle John says that he and the other disciples 'beheld' the glory of God in Jesus Christ. Using the Scripture references write in the blanks on the left the places where the glory of God was revealed and on the right the ones to whom it was revealed.

Places		Persons
_____	(Luke 2:8-9)	_____
_____	(John 2:1,11)	_____
_____	(Luke 9:28,32)	_____
_____	(John 11:1,4,14-45)	_____

The answers to the questions relating to this and the other chapters in this book can be found on the EP Books web site at www.epbooks.org.

 Just type the title of this book in the 'Quick Find' box, then click on 'Answers' to find the relevant entries.

Three days

'The next day John saw Jesus coming toward him, and said, "Behold! The Lamb of God who takes away the sin of the world!"' (1:29).

In these verses, the apostle John begins to relate the actual events of Jesus' life and ministry by presenting the witness of John the Baptist.

> 'The greatest saints of God in every age of the Church have always been men of John the Baptist's spirit. In gifts, and knowledge, and general character they have often differed widely. But in one respect they have always been alike: they have been "clothed with humility" (1 Peter 5:5). They have not sought their own honour. They have thought little of themselves. They have been ever willing to decrease if Christ might only increase, to be nothing if Christ might be all'
> (J. C. Ryle, *Expository Thoughts on John*, vol. 1, p.45).

One day: John answers questions about himself (vv. 19-28)

The questioners (vv. 19,24,28)

John the Baptist was baptizing in Bethabara (v. 28), which was situated about twenty miles east of Jerusalem on the Jordan

River, when he received a delegation of priests and Levites (v. 19), both of whom had responsibilities in the temple in Jerusalem. This delegation was sent by 'the Jews' (v. 19), the apostle John's term for the religious leaders, whom he also identifies as 'the Pharisees' (v. 24).

The questions (vv. 19-23,25-27)

1. *'Who are you?'* (vv. 19-23). The ministry of John the Baptist had created such a stir among the people that many of them had concluded that he was either the Messiah, the prophet Elijah or the great prophet predicted by Moses (Deut. 18:15-18). The Pharisees, ever concerned about maintaining their hold on the people, wanted to know if John made any of these claims for himself.

John responded to this question by stating clearly that he was not the Messiah, Elijah or the prophet (vv. 20-21), but was rather the one who had been sent by God to announce the coming of the Messiah. In filling this role, John was fulfilling Isaiah's prophecy (Isa. 40:3).

2. *'Why then do you baptize...?'* (vv. 25-27). The Pharisees were evidently willing to grant that the Messiah, Elijah or the great prophet would have the authority to baptize, but they were not willing to grant that same authority to John.

Some think that John refused to explain why he baptized. They contend that he rather pointed to the Messiah, essentially saying, 'Instead of being concerned about me, you should be concerned about the Messiah who is about to appear. I am nothing at all compared to him.'

In other words, John was telling them that there was someone of real value in their midst, but it was not he.

'It will be better at the last day never to have been born, than to have had Christ "standing among us" and not to have known Him'

(J. C. Ryle, *Thoughts*, vol. 1, p.47).

Others think that in pointing to the Messiah, John was explaining that his baptizing was designed to prepare the way for Christ (v. 31). John's baptism was one of repentance, and the only way Christ can be received is through true repentance.

The next day: John announces the Lord Jesus Christ (vv. 29-34)

As the Lamb of God (v. 29)

When John the Baptist saw Jesus coming toward him, he cried out: 'Behold! The Lamb of God who takes away the sin of the world!' With these words, John not only identified Jesus as the Messiah, but also clearly indicated that, as the Messiah, he would not set up a political kingdom but rather offer himself as a sacrifice for sinners.

'Without any exception, every kind of sin and evil is covered. There is no sin too heinous, no wickedness too terrible, no habitual failure too often repeated that it cannot be "taken away" by Christ, our heavenly Lamb'

(Bruce Milne, *The Message of John*, p.54).

As his superior (vv. 30-31)

1. *In time* (v. 30). After declaring Jesus to be the Lamb of God, John proceeded to offer something of a riddle, that is, Jesus was at one and the same time after him and before

him. Jesus was after John in terms of his appearance on the stage of human history, or, in terms of public ministry. But Jesus came before John in that he, Jesus, did not begin to exist when he was born of Mary. He was nothing less than the eternal God in human flesh.

2. *In baptism* (vv. 31-34). John came baptizing in water in order to pave the way for Jesus who would baptize with the Spirit. The water was the sign of the Spirit and John could only administer the sign. Jesus alone could administer the Spirit himself, and his cleansing power.

Because it had been revealed to him by God, John the Baptist knew Jesus was the Messiah. This revelation evidently occurred when John saw Jesus approaching (v. 29), and it was confirmed by the Holy Spirit descending upon Jesus in the form of a dove (vv. 32-33, cf. Matt. 3:16; Mark 1:10).

Some are troubled by John's statement that he did not know Jesus because the two were cousins. However, John was merely saying that he did not know Jesus was the Messiah until this time.

The third day: John repeats his announcement (vv. 35-37)

In order that the two disciples (Andrew and John) would follow Jesus, John the Baptist identified him as the Lamb of God. The Baptist always kept in mind that his ministry was not to gather followers for himself but for Christ.

'Those who have said the most honourable things of Christ will never see cause to unsay them; but the more they know him the more they are confirmed in their esteem of him'
(Matthew Henry, *Commentary*, vol. v, p.862).

The Christ identified by John is still the Lamb of God. As such, he and he alone is the sacrifice for our sins. He is also worthy of the same zeal and devotion given him by John the Baptist.

DIGGING DEEPER

1. *Read verses 19-28. What admirable qualities did John the Baptist manifest?*

2. *Read verse 20. Identify someone from the Bible who had the opportunity to do as John the Baptist did but chose to deny and not confess.*

3. *Read verse 29. How did John the Baptist identify Jesus? Read Exodus 12:1-7. How does Jesus take away sin? Read Hebrews 9:26 and 1 Peter 2:24.*

4. *Read Revelation 5:6-14. How is Jesus identified in these verses? What words of praise are offered to him by his people?*

5. *Read verse 34. How did John the Baptist identify Jesus here? What does this tell you about the person of Jesus?*

Unscramble the following words to find a statement from Matthew Henry:

stcirh   ilwl   tehier   kaet uro   nsis   ywaa ro   etka

_____ ____ _____ _____ ____ _____ _____ ___ _____

su   waya.

____ _____.

The claiming Christ

'And he said to him, "Most assuredly, I say to you, hereafter you shall see heaven open, and the angels of God ascending and descending upon the Son of Man"' (1:51).

These verses give us the apostle John's account of how Jesus called the first five of his original twelve disciples. When we lay John's description alongside the other Gospel records on this matter, we are forced to draw the conclusion that there were several stages in the formation of the twelve. They were already men of faith, having embraced the Old Testament promises regarding the Messiah. Here Jesus calls them to embrace him as the fulfilment of those promises.

The particularly fascinating aspect of John's record is how Jesus dealt with these men as individuals. From this we can conclude that while there is only one way of salvation — faith in the finished work of the Lord Jesus Christ — there are many ways in which people come to that faith.

'There are diversities of operations in the saving of souls. All true Christians are led by one Spirit, washed in one blood, serve one Lord, lean on one Saviour, believe one truth, and walk by one general rule. But all are not converted in one and the same manner. All do not pass through the same experience. In conversion, the Holy Ghost acts as a sovereign. He calleth every one severally as He will'

(J. C. Ryle, *Thoughts*, vol. 1, p.78).

We must always be careful that we do not make one experience of conversion the pattern for all. Some weep when they come to Christ, but others do not. Some come quickly to Christ, but others come only after a prolonged struggle.

The men whom Jesus claimed

We must also resist the temptation to make the men with whom Jesus dealt the main characters of this story. That place is reserved for the Lord Jesus who claimed and conquered them.

John and Andrew (vv. 35-39)

Although Andrew alone is specifically identified as one of the disciples of John the Baptist (v. 40), we may rest assured that the author of this Gospel was the other. Throughout this Gospel John cloaks himself in secrecy.

John and Andrew can be described as seekers. The fact that they had been following John the Baptist indicated that they were eagerly looking forward to the coming of the Messiah. It is not surprising that they began to follow Jesus very soon after John the Baptist identified him.

Simon Peter (v. 42)

Peter was an ordinary man. He was also very emotional and could rapidly change from one mood to another. He may very well have thought his personality would preclude the Messiah from having any interest in him.

Philip (vv. 43-44)

John's later references to Philip (6:7; 14:8) suggest that he was a practical, hard-nosed businessman who sought to analyse every detail before committing himself to a particular course of action. He may very well have been so occupied with business that he had little time for talk of the Messiah.

Nathaniel (v. 46)

Nathaniel appears to have been a doubting, sceptical man who could not easily be convinced or won over. He may have been highly intellectual. Because Jesus came from Nazareth, Nathaniel ruled out any possibility that he could be the Messiah. He may have come to this conclusion on the basis of Micah's prophecy about Bethlehem (Micah 5:2); or he may have assumed that it was impossible for the Messiah to hail from a village so common and unappealing as Nazareth.

The means by which Jesus claimed them

John and Andrew

John and Andrew were claimed through the preaching of John the Baptist (vv. 36-37). This is the avenue by which the vast majority of believers come to know the Lord Jesus Christ. The apostle Paul says, 'Faith comes by hearing, and hearing by the word of God' (Rom. 10:17).

But not just any preaching will do. It must be preaching like that of John the Baptist, that is, preaching that points to Jesus Christ as the only sufficient sacrifice for sin.

All preachers should take comfort from these verses. The first day John the Baptist proclaimed Jesus as the Lamb of God, no one responded. This was the second day he made the proclamation and John and Andrew responded.

31

Simon Peter and Nathaniel

Simon Peter and Nathaniel were claimed through personal witnessing. Andrew '…first found his own brother… And he brought him to Jesus' (vv. 41-42). In like manner, Philip, after meeting Jesus, went to share the good news with Nathaniel (v. 45).

We should take the word 'first' (v. 41) to mean as 'a matter of first importance'. Have those of us who know Christ considered it a matter of first importance to witness to our own family members?

> 'The work of testifying the Gospel of the grace of God ought not to be left to ministers alone. All who have received mercy ought to find a tongue, and to declare what God has done for their souls … Thousands, humanly speaking, would listen to a word from a friend, who will not listen to a sermon. Every believer ought to be a home-missionary — a missionary to his family, children, servants, neighbours, and friends. Surely, if we can find nothing to say to others about Jesus, we may well doubt whether we are savingly acquainted with Him ourselves'
>
> (J. C. Ryle, *Thoughts*, vol. 1, p.72).

Philip

Philip was claimed by means of Jesus' sovereign intervention and call (v. 43). While all conversions result from the sovereign grace of God, there are instances in which God displays that grace more fully by bringing salvation without using human instruments. We have one example of this when Jesus authoritatively summons Philip with the words: 'Follow me.' Saul of Tarsus is the classic example of this type of conversion (Acts 9:1-9).

The attributes Jesus displayed in claiming them

A tender and kind spirit (v. 39)

Jesus welcomed Andrew and John by inviting them to spend time with him and to get acquainted with him.

'...He knew their desires. He had read their hearts. He discerned that they sought His presence, His person, His fellowship. And He never disappoints *such* longings'
(Arthur W. Pink,
Exposition of the Gospel of John, vol. i, p.69).

Sovereign authority and grace (vv. 42-43)

To give someone a new name, as Jesus did with Simon (v. 42), indicates authority over that person. As noted above, Jesus displayed that same authority in calling Philip (v. 43).

It was sovereign authority that *could* do these things. It was grace that *would* do these things. How persistently that grace would work in the life of the impetuous Simon to mould him into a mature saint!

Divine knowledge (vv. 47-51)

Nathaniel's scepticism melted when Jesus said, 'Before Philip called you, when you were under the fig tree, I saw you' (v. 48).

If Jesus had seen him, he had to have knowledge from above. He must, therefore, be from above. On the basis of the knowledge Jesus had revealed, Nathaniel could do nothing but believe the promise Jesus made that Nathaniel would see heaven open and angels ascending and descending upon him, Jesus. Nathaniel would indeed see Jesus bringing heaven to earth and the signature of heaven upon his ministry.

'It is interesting that Nathaniel had nothing to say about Nazareth. He still did not know how Nazareth fitted into this puzzle, but he could not allow what he did not know to obscure what he did know. This Jesus was the Messiah. There could be no other explanation for him. Nathaniel could wait to find out about Nazareth, but he could not wait to confess the faith that flooded into his heart. Christians do not believe in Christ because he has given them the answer to every single question that has cropped up in their minds but rather because they have encountered overwhelming evidence that he is indeed God in human flesh'

(Roger Ellsworth,
How to Live in a Dangerous World, p.119).

Twice in this passage we encounter the words 'Come and see' (vv. 39,46). It does not matter whether one is an active seeker like John and Andrew, an ordinary person like Simon Peter, or a doubter like Nathaniel — he who comes to Christ will find him to be the satisfying Saviour.

DIGGING DEEPER

1. *Read verses 37-39. How did Jesus respond to Andrew and John? What does this tell you about Jesus?*

2. *Read verses 40-42. How did Simon Peter come to Jesus? What promise did Jesus make to him?*

3. *Read verses 43-46. On what basis did Nathaniel conclude that Jesus could not be the Messiah? What preconceived ideas do people have today that keep them from Christ?*

4. *Read verses 47-48. How did Jesus convince Nathaniel that he, Jesus, was the Messiah? Why do you think Nathaniel refused to bring up the subject of Nazareth?*

5. *Read verses 49-51. Compare these verses with Genesis 28:10-12. Was Jesus claiming to be the ladder to heaven? What does a ladder represent?*

Use the first letters of the missing words in the verses below to arrive at one of the keys words in this week's lesson:

`_____out your own salvation with fear and trembling' (Phil. 2:13).

'The wise shall _____glory' (Prov. 3:35).

' I _____in the mercy of God' (Ps. 52:8).

'do all in the _____of the Lord Jesus' (Col. 3:17).

'the truth of the Lord _____for ever' (Ps. 117:2).

'For even the Son of Man did not come to be _____, but to _____' (Mark 10:45).

KEY WORD: ___ ___ ___ ___ ___ ___ ___

WEEK 4
John 2:1-11

The beginning of Jesus' signs

 'This beginning of signs Jesus did in Cana of Galilee, and manifested his glory; and his disciples believed in him' (2:11).

Jesus' first miracle was performed in Cana. John specifies that this was a town in Galilee, but its precise location is unknown. The time of this miracle was 'on the third day' (v. 1), that is, the third day after Jesus called Philip and Nathaniel (1:43-51).

'After thirty years' seclusion at Nazareth, He now for the first time lifted up the veil which He had thrown over His divinity in becoming flesh, and revealed something of His almighty power and Godhead'

(J. C. Ryle, *Thoughts*, vol. 1, p.102).

Why did Jesus attend the feast in Cana? The following answers have been suggested:

1. to show that he could enter into the joys of life;
2. to set his stamp of approval upon marriage;
3. to show his concern for even the trivial details of life.

'...it is most significant ... that his first miracle ... was so related to the joy of a wedding feast. It rebukes the foolish fear that religion robs life of its happiness, or that loyalty to Christ is inconsistent with exuberant spirits and innocent pleasure. It corrects the false impression that sourness is a sign of sainthood, or that gloom is a condition of godliness'

(Charles R. Erdman,
An Exposition: The Gospel of John, p.29).

Mary reports the situation to Jesus (vv. 3-5)

Wine, a symbol of joy (Judges 9:13; Ps. 104:15; Eccles. 10:19), was considered essential for such a happy occasion. It was no small thing, therefore, when the wine ran out. Such a calamity may even have been viewed as an ill omen for the young couple. Mary knew what to do about this dilemma. She reported it to Jesus in these simple words: 'They have no wine.' Jesus' response to Mary indicates that she had more on her mind than the wine.

'What Mary seemed to desire was that her Son should take this occasion to manifest himself openly as the Messiah, and she mentions the need of wine as her reason for suggesting such a Messianic manifestation'

(Charles R. Erdman, *The Gospel of John*, p.28).

Jesus answered Mary in this way: 'Woman, what does your concern have to do with me? My hour has not yet come' (v. 4). We should note the following about his response:

1. By using the word 'woman', Jesus was not being rude. Our equivalent to this would be 'dear lady'. With this term Jesus intended to convey both affection and distance. While Jesus loved Mary, it was necessary for her to recognize that he was much more than her son.

2. The time was not right for him to reveal himself as the Messiah.

'He had a clear idea of the timetable for his mission as the Saviour of his people. At the beginning, Jesus took care to conceal his glory so as not to draw the unwelcome attention of his enemies until the time was ripe'

(Gordon J. Keddie,
A Study Commentary on John, vol. 1, p.105).

Mary's response to Jesus (v. 5) shows that she understood his point and was willing to leave the matter to him. It confirms that she had genuine faith.

Jesus addresses the situation (vv. 6-8)

While Jesus rejected Mary's desire for him to openly claim messiahship, he did not reject her request for help. He commanded that six waterpots be filled with water (v. 7). Then he said: 'Draw some out now, and take it to the master of the feast' (v. 8).

The apostle John found particular significance in the fact that the waterpots Jesus used were for the ceremonial cleansings required by Judaism (v. 6). The fact that Jesus transformed the water in those pots indicated that what he had come to do would surpass Judaism even as wine surpasses water.

The law of Moses, which was the centrepiece of Judaism, was not given by God for the purpose of bringing salvation. It was rather given so we would become keenly conscious of how impossible it is for us to attain salvation by our own efforts and to drive us, therefore, to look forward in faith to the coming Christ. The fact that Christ was there in Cana and would soon go to the cross meant that the purpose for which the law had been given was completely fulfilled.

Here Jesus manifested power to change something into that which was totally and radically different. This proved that he was no ordinary man, but was, as John has already testified, filled with the glory of the only begotten of the Father (1:18).

We cannot ponder Jesus' power to change without thinking of salvation. There is no more radical change, and it comes about only through the power of Jesus. Mary said of the people at the feast: 'They have no wine.' There was a point at which it could be said of all believers: 'They have no life.' But the power of Jesus that changed water into wine changed our deadness into life (2 Cor. 5:17; Eph. 2:1-10).

'I am reminded of the story of the drunken coal miner who was converted and became a vocal witness for Christ. One of his friends tried to trap him by asking, "Do you believe that Jesus turned water into wine?"

'"I certainly do!" the believer replied. "In my home, He has turned wine into furniture, decent clothes, and food for my children!"'

(Warren W. Wiersbe,
The Bible Exposition Commentary, vol. i, p.292).

The master of the feast responds (vv. 9-10)

When the master of the feast tasted the wine, he essentially said to the bridegroom, 'You have saved the best for last.' While salvation offers many benefits and blessings in this world, these things cannot begin to compare to the glory that awaits believers in heaven (Rom. 8:18; 2 Cor. 4:16-18).

The apostle reports the effect of this miracle (v. 11)

John tells us that Jesus used this miracle to manifest his glory and, in doing so, caused his believing disciples to believe even more (v. 11).

'A greater marriage feast than that of Cana will one day be held, when Christ Himself will be the bridegroom and believers will be the bride. A greater glory will one day be manifested, when Jesus shall take to Himself His great power and reign. Blessed will they be in that day who are called to the marriage supper of the Lamb!'

(J. C. Ryle, *Thoughts*, vol. 1, p.94).

DIGGING DEEPER

1. *Read verses 1-2. What can we conclude about Jesus from his willingness to attend a wedding?*

2. *Read verses 3-5. What do these verses tell us about Mary?*

3. *Read verses 6-8. These verses tell us that Jesus has transforming power. What are some other instances in which Jesus demonstrated such power?*

4. *Read verses 9-10. What do these verses teach us about the kind of work that Jesus does?*

5. *Read verse 11. Is it not true to say that Jesus' disciples already believed? What are we to understand, then, from this verse?*

Jesus performed his first miracle at Cana. Look up John's accounts of six more of Jesus' miracles. In the blanks on the left describe what Jesus did. In the blanks on the right, write the place where each miracle was performed:

_____ (4:46-54)   _____

_____ (5:1-9)   _____

_____ (6:1-14)   _____

_____ (6:15-21)   _____

_____ (9:1-7)   _____

_____ (11:38-44) _____

WEEK 5

John 2:12-25

Jesus cleanses the temple

 'Then his disciples remembered that it was written, "Zeal for your house has eaten me up"' (2:17).

John here begins to relate some of the details of Jesus' first visit to Jerusalem after he began his public ministry. He first mentions Jesus' brief stay in Capernaum (v. 12).

'Jesus was waiting for the passover; he knew always when his "hour" was come; he was also selecting a more convenient center than Nazareth for his public ministry. This verse marks the transition from his private to his public career'
(Charles R. Erdman, *John*, p.31).

John's record of this visit to Jerusalem consists of three things:

1. Jesus cleansing the temple (2:13-22);
2. Jesus rejecting some would-be disciples (vv. 23-25);
3. Jesus visiting with Nicodemus (3:1-21).

The first two of these events is presented in the verses of today's lesson.

Jesus cleanses the temple (vv. 13-22)

The setting for this action

The Passover was the greatest of the Jewish festivals. It commemorated the night the angel of death 'passed over' the firstborn of the nation of Israel. This had occurred when the Israelites had sacrificed lambs as substitutes for the firstborn and placed the blood of those lambs on their houses. All those in houses with blood on the doorposts were safe from the sentence of condemnation (Exod. 11:1 - 12:30).

The Passover was, therefore, a time for the people to reflect with deep gratitude on what God had done in the past and to offer sacrifices.

The reason for this action

The Passover was also a time of terrible abuse. Because it brought thousands of pilgrims to Jerusalem, some people took the opportunity to make a lot of money. Many of the pilgrims would come without an animal for sacrifice. Others would bring animals only to have the inspectors find flaws that made those animals unacceptable for sacrifice. So animals were kept on hand for worshippers who needed them; but the prices were exorbitant.

Another abuse arose as a result of the temple tax, which had to be paid in Jewish currency. When worshippers came to Jerusalem from other lands, their currency had to be exchanged. This service was also performed at the temple, but, again, at a substantial cost.

It was quite a scene that greeted Jesus when he arrived at the outer court of the temple. Sheep were bleating and bawling. Merchants were barking out their prices. The stench of excrement was everywhere. There was nothing there to indicate or to encourage worship.

44

Overwhelmed with indignation and with zeal for his 'Father's house' (v. 16), Jesus made 'a whip of cords' (v. 15) and 'drove them all out of the temple' (v. 15), overturning the tables of the moneychangers in the process (v. 15). Gordon J. Keddie says of Jesus:

'He wants an end to greed and corruption and the secularizing spirit of the age in our lives, our churches and our communities and nations. He wants repentance from the worldliness, covenant-breaking and backsliding that in effect deny Christ and tell the world we really have no life-changing message, no powerful gospel, at all'

(*John*, vol. 1, p.120).

The results of this action

1. *The disciples were impressed* (v. 17). What Jesus did reminded his disciples of the words of Psalm 69:9. That verse, from one of the messianic psalms, had been fulfilled before their eyes.

The zeal of Jesus for the temple should cause all of us to consider how much zeal we have for the church and its worship. One of the things we must learn from this episode is that Jesus highly values worship and insists that it be done in the right way. What is acceptable worship? It is that which is in accordance with what God has revealed — reverent and God-honouring. Bruce Milne applies Jesus' cleansing of the temple in this way:

'Modern-day worship which is irreverent, superficial, distraction-filled, cold, lifeless, sloppy, self-indulgent, hypocritical, ill-prepared or theologically inappropriate will likewise receive his censure, as will worship which detracts from the honour and glory of the living God through a concern for performance and self-display on the part of those leading it'

(Bruce Milne, *The Message of John*, pp.70-1).

2. *The religious leaders were indignant* (vv. 18-21). By demanding a sign, these men were asking Jesus to prove that he had the authority to do what he had done.

> '...this request was *stupid*. The temple-cleansing was itself a sign. It was a definite anticipatory fulfillment of Mal. 3:1-3 ("The Lord whom ye seek will suddenly come to his temple … he will purify the sons of Levi")...
>
> 'The request for a sign was not only stupid, however; it was also *wicked*. It was the result of unwillingness to admit guilt. The authorities should have been ashamed of all this graft and greed within the temple-court. Instead of asking Jesus by what right he had cleansed the temple, they should have confessed their sins and thanked him'
>
> (William Hendriksen, *New Testament Commentary: John*, vol. i, p.124, italics are his).

Jesus gave them an answer that baffled them (v. 19). His authority lay in his ability to build a destroyed temple in three days. They were astonished because they assumed he was speaking of that building which had been under construction for forty-six years. The disciples, who were taking all this in, would come to understand later that he was referring to the temple of his body, which he did raise up three days after it was destroyed, that is, after he had died.

> 'In raising Himself from the dead He would furnish the final proof that He was God manifest in flesh, and if God, then the One Who possessed the unequivocal right to cleanse the defiled temple which bore His name'
>
> (Arthur W. Pink, *Exposition of the Gospel of John*, vol. i, p.99).

Jesus rejects would-be disciples (vv. 23-25)

These verses present us with a sad and deeply disturbing reality, namely, it is possible to have a certain kind of belief in Jesus which falls short of true belief.

While in Jerusalem for the Passover, Jesus performed some miracles. These caused many to believe in him (v. 23). But John says Jesus 'did not commit himself to them' (v. 24). Because he perfectly knew all men and did not need any help in discerning the inner workings of human minds and hearts, Jesus could easily see that these people did not have true and genuine faith. They evidently believed in him only as a miracle-worker and not as the God-man and the Saviour of sinners.

Scripture indicates that a great number will go through this life thinking they have true faith only to discover that they were sadly mistaken (Matt. 7:21-23).

DIGGING DEEPER

1. *Read verses 12-13. Locate Capernaum and Jerusalem on a map of Palestine during the time of Jesus.*

2. *Read verse 13. What does Jesus' attendance at the Passover and his going to the temple tell us about his religious habits?*

3. *Read verses 14-16. What do these verses tell us about Jesus?*

4. *Read verses 17-20. Jesus' action caused the disciples to think of Psalm 69:9. What does this tell us about these men? What does the inability of the religious leaders to understand Jesus' words tell us about them?*

5. *Read verses 19-22. What does the resurrection of Jesus tell us about him?*

6. *Read verses 23-25. Think of other biblical examples of people who appeared to have true faith but did not. Who among Jesus' disciples was in this category?*

The Synoptic Gospels record another instance of Jesus cleansing the temple. This occurred during the week that ended in his crucifixion (Matt. 21:12-16; Mark 11:15-18; Luke 19:45-48). Write in the blanks provided the letters 'S' for features that are included in the Synoptic Gospels and 'J' for features found in John's Gospel.

_____   den of thieves
_____   a whip of cords
_____   eaten by zeal for the Lord's house
_____   the Jews demanding a sign
_____   house of prayer

Jesus and Nicodemus

'For God so loved the world that he gave his only begotten Son, that whoever believes in him should not perish but have everlasting life' (3:16).

Nicodemus was a very intelligent and influential man. He was a Pharisee and a ruler of the Jews (v. 1). He was also honoured and noted as a teacher (v. 10). In addition to these things, it is very probable that he was quite wealthy.

As a devout Jew, Nicodemus was living in eager expectation of the Messiah's coming. The miracles that Jesus had been performing left no doubt in his mind that Jesus had been sent by God (v. 2). He evidently came seeking confirmation that Jesus was indeed the Messiah. He received vital information about what was necessary for him to enter Jesus' kingdom and why he should listen to Jesus' words. In other words, Nicodemus received teaching about spiritual birth and about Jesus as a teacher.

Jesus talks about spiritual birth (vv. 3-8)

Indispensable for entering the kingdom of God (v. 3)

Jesus did not object to Nicodemus calling him 'a teacher come from God'. He rather used the opportunity to draw his attention to the purpose for which he, Jesus, had been sent. He essentially said, 'You say I am sent from God. Let me tell you why.'

Jesus was sent to provide the way for sinners to enter heaven. Nicodemus wanted Jesus to confirm his messiahship. Nicodemus assumed that he, by virtue of being a Jew, would automatically be part of the Messiah's kingdom. Imagine his shock when he learned that Jesus' kingdom was not of this world and could only be entered by means of a spiritual birth! Just as we have no knowledge or experience of physical life until we are born into it, so we have no knowledge or experience of spiritual life until we are born into it.

'A day will come when those who are not born again will wish that they had never been born at all'
(J. C. Ryle, *Thoughts*, vol. 1, p.125).

Initiated and produced by God (vv. 3-7)

Nicodemus wondered how such a birth could take place again (vv. 3-4).

'It is as if Nicodemus said with infinite, wistful yearning: "You talk about being born again; you talk about this radical fundamental change which is so necessary. I know that it is necessary; but in my experience it is so *impossible*. There is nothing I would like more; but you might as well tell me, a full grown man, to enter into my mother's womb and to be born all over again." It is not the *desirability* of this change that Nicodemus questioned; that he knew only too well; it is the *possibility*. Nicodemus is up against the eternal problem, the problem of the man who wants to be changed, and who cannot change himself'
(William Barclay, *The Gospel of John*, vol. i, p.114, italics are his).

But Jesus was talking about a birth that was of 'water and the Spirit' (v. 5). Because water is used in Scripture as an emblem of the Word of God (Ps. 119:9; Eph. 5:26), we should understand that the spiritual birth is produced by the Spirit of God using the Word of God or making the teachings of God's Word effective in the heart of the unbeliever (Rom. 10:17; Eph. 6:17; James 1:18; 1 Peter 1:23).

> 'This mighty change, it must never be forgotten, we cannot give to ourselves. The very name which our Lord gives to it is a convincing proof of this. He calls it "a birth". No man is the author of his own existence, and no man can quicken his own soul. We might as well expect a dead man to give himself life, as expect a natural man to make himself spiritual. A power from above must be put in exercise, even that same power which created the world (2 Cor. iv. 6). Man can do many things; but he cannot give life either to himself or to others. To give life is the peculiar prerogative of God'
> (J. C. Ryle, *Thoughts*, vol. 1, p.123).

> 'The new birth is a secret work of God, in which the Holy Spirit works according to his hidden power and secret will. The new birth is not predictable, because it is a sovereign work of God's grace. It is not an act of the human will, because it is effected by the Holy Spirit in a heart that is opposed to the very idea. It is *all* the work of God'
> (Gordon J. Keddie, *John*, vol. 1, p.132, italics are his).

Noticeable results (v. 8)

Just as our physical birth results in us having the nature of our parents, so spiritual birth results in us having a new nature, a spiritual nature that evidences itself just as the wind evidences itself. What does this say about those who hold to the 'carnal Christian' teaching which asserts that it is possible to be saved and live as the unsaved?

Jesus talks about himself and his mission (vv. 9-21)

He came from heaven with heaven's authority (vv. 9-13)

Jesus was not speaking as one more in a long line of religious teachers. He spoke as a reliable authority because he had first-hand knowledge of heavenly things — because he came from heaven (vv. 11,13). It was impossible for Nicodemus or anyone else to ascend to heaven and secure information about the new birth, but it was not impossible for Jesus to come down to earth from heaven (v. 13).

> '...the truths of Christ are of undoubted certainty. We have all the reasons in the world to be assured that the sayings of Christ are *faithful sayings*, and such as we may venture our souls upon; for he is not only a *credible* witness, who would not go about to deceive us, but a *competent* witness, who could not himself be deceived'
> (Matthew Henry, vol. v, p.885, italics are his).

He came from heaven to make spiritual birth possible (vv. 14-17)

The spiritual birth of which Jesus had been speaking could not take place apart from the completion of his mission which he would accomplish by dying on the cross. In these verses, Jesus points Nicodemus to the cross.

1. *Jesus' death was designed to deal with sin* (v. 14). God commanded Moses to lift up the serpent in the wilderness as the remedy for the sin of Israel (Num. 21:4-9). Jesus would

be lifted up on the cross to make atonement for sin. Spiritual birth is life that is granted to us by God himself through his Spirit and his Word. God could not grant us life until something was done about our sins. God has said from the beginning that sin brings death.

God could not simply ignore our sin. His holy character made that impossible. God has to punish sin or cease to be God. How, then, could God at one and the same time punish sinners with eternal death and yet give them spiritual and eternal life? The cross is the answer. There God punished sin in Christ and provided the way for sinners to have eternal life.

2. *Jesus' death expressed the love of God* (vv. 16-17). What marvellous love is manifested by the cross of Christ! It is marvellous because it was given by an unspeakably glorious person (God), to unspeakably needy people (perishing), at an unspeakably great cost (only begotten Son), to bestow an unspeakably great benefit (everlasting life).

3. *Jesus' death must be appropriated by faith* (vv. 15-21). The word 'believe' carries with it the element of commitment. It is not just agreeing that Jesus actually lived and that he died on the cross, but rather relying on him and his death for our eternal salvation.

The entire human race is divided into two groups: those who have genuine faith in Christ and those who do not. Why are so many in this latter group? The truth about Jesus Christ shines like light, but everyone comes into this world with a nature that loves the darkness of sin. Those who love darkness cannot love light. How then can anyone come to the light? No one can, apart from God working within him and enabling him to do so. The one who comes to the light manifests or proves in the very act of coming that God has been working in him.

DIGGING   DEEPER

1. *Read verses 1-2. What information do these verses give us about Nicodemus?*

2. *Read verses 3-8. What is necessary to enter the kingdom of God? What kind of kingdom did Nicodemus have in mind?*

3. *Read verse 8. As the wind produces effects, so does spiritual birth. Name some of those effects.*

4. *Read verses 9-13. What does Jesus say about himself in these verses?*

5. *Read verse 14. To what is Jesus referring here?*

6. *Read verses 15-16. What is necessary to have eternal life?*

7. *Read verse 17. Why did Jesus come?*

8. *Read verses 18-21. What do these verses teach about the condition of people apart from Christ?*

Read the following verses and write in the blank provided the phrase that occurs in each:
1 John 3:9; 4:7; 5:1,4,18

_____.

The last testimony of John the Baptist

'He who believes in the Son has everlasting life; and he who does not believe the Son shall not see life, but the wrath of God abides on him' (3:36).

After celebrating the Passover in Jerusalem, Jesus and his disciples spent some time in the countryside of Judea. There they conducted a ministry much like that of John the Baptist, who was himself still active (vv. 23-24). Jesus himself did not baptize (4:1-2) but authorized his disciples to do so on his behalf.

The jealousy of John the Baptist's disciples (vv. 22-26)

The fact that Jesus' ministry began to surpass John's (4:1) brought distress to some of the latter's disciples (v. 26). This distress was precipitated by their conversation with 'the Jews', the religious leaders (v. 25), who may very well have suggested that the success of Jesus indicated that the baptism he offered must be superior to that of John the Baptist. The words of the Baptist's disciples suggest that they thought Jesus was showing lack of gratitude and respect to John.

'The true Christian must watch and pray against the spirit here manifested by John's disciples... Nothing so defiles Christianity and gives the enemies of truth such occasion to blaspheme, as jealousy and party-spirit among Christians. Wherever there is real grace, we should be ready and willing to acknowledge it, even though it may be outside our own pale'

(J. C. Ryle, *Thoughts*, vol. 1, pp.171-2).

The humility of John the Baptist (vv. 27-30)

The response of John the Baptist shows us the type of spirit all God's people should have, that is, the spirit of meekness and humility. We can divide his answer into four parts.

A general principle (v. 27)

John the Baptist knew that the increase of Jesus' ministry and the decrease of his own were not to be explained in terms of luck or technique. It was rather a matter of divine sovereignty. God is in control, and he determines the roles of his servants. To complain about the role of another is, therefore, to complain about the decision-making of the very one we are supposed to revere and serve.

'The herald of Christ meant to say that to every one God has assigned a place in his eternal plan, and that he, the Baptist, has no right to lay claim to an honor which had not been given to him in heaven'

(William Hendriksen, vol. i, p.148).

A gentle reminder (v. 28)

John calls upon his disciples to remember what they themselves had heard him say from the beginning, namely, he was not the Messiah but was sent to announce the Messiah.

A clear illustration (v. 29)

Here John the Baptist uses wedding imagery to convey the nature of his relationship to Jesus. The best man in the wedding does not rush up and take the bride when she is presented to the groom. He is content merely to stand beside the groom and rejoice in hearing him speak to the bride. John the Baptist knew that the Lord Jesus was already in the process of receiving his bride (his people), and he was glad to see it.

An inevitable conclusion (v. 30)

Believing in those things which he sets forth in verses 27-29, John the Baptist could only desire to see the Lord Jesus increase. The ancient herald who announced the coming of the king would have been the centre of attention for a while. People would have been milling around him with great excitement. But when the king arrived, all the attention would be diverted to him. John the Baptist was the herald. Jesus was the king who had now arrived.

The words of John the Baptist did not fit his situation alone. Every Christian should deliberately and gladly embrace them as a fitting and unchanging motto.

The supremacy of Jesus (vv. 31-36)

Some commentators regard these verses as a continuation of the remarks of John the Baptist. Others think that the Baptist's words end with verse 30, and these are the words of the author of this Gospel. No matter which position we take, the message remains the same, and that is, of course, the supremacy of Christ.

> 'We can never make too much of Christ… He is worthy of all the honour that we can give Him. He will be all in heaven. Let us see to it, that He is all in our hearts on earth'
>
> (J. C. Ryle, vol. 1, p.174).

We can summarize the message of these verses with four main statements:

1. *Christ is above all because he came from above* (v. 31). No one else has come to this world from heaven as Jesus did. No other is entitled, therefore, to our worship and obedience. But he is!

2. *Christ is above all because his teaching is above all* (vv. 32-34). The Lord Jesus came to speak about things of which he had first-hand knowledge (v. 32), that is, the things of heaven. How sad it is that so many reject his testimony — as if they knew more than he! The words of Jesus are also to be believed because God gave him the fulness of the Holy Spirit (v. 34).

3. *Christ is above all because his authority comes from above* (v. 35).

4. *Christ is above all because he is the difference between going above and going below* (v. 36). There are no plainer words on the matter of salvation than those in this verse. Those who commit themselves to Christ have eternal life. Those who do not commit to Christ have eternal wrath abiding on them.

DIGGING DEEPER

1. *Read verses 22-25. What facts do these verses give us?*

2. *Read verse 26. What was the complaint of the disciples of John the Baptist?*

3. *Read verses 27-30. What do these verses tell us about the character of John the Baptist?*

4. *Read verses 31-36. What do these verses tell us about the Lord Jesus Christ? What should we do in light of these things?*

 Missionary Jim Elliott, who was killed by the Auca Indians in Ecuador in 1956, serves as a good example of one who believed Christ is 'above all' (v. 31). Find in the following verses of Scripture the words to complete Elliott's much loved statement:

'He is no _____ [Luke 12:20] who gives up what he cannot _____ [John 14:15] to _____ [Dan. 2:8] what he cannot _____ [Luke 17:33].'

WEEK 8
John 4:1-26

Jesus and the Samaritan woman

'God is Spirit, and those who worship him must worship in spirit and truth' (4:24).

In 722 B.C. the Assyrians invaded the land of Israel and carried many of its citizens into captivity. These people, for the most part, were absorbed into Assyria and never returned.

The land of Israel, on the other hand, was populated with those who were not taken captive and with people from foreign lands whom the Assyrians brought in. It was not long before the Israelites began to inter-marry with the other people, creating a mixed race which became known as the Samaritans.

In 586 B.C. the Babylonians invaded the land of Judah and carried many of her citizens into captivity. The people of Judah, unlike those of Israel, did not lose their identity. They returned to their homeland under the leadership of Ezra and Nehemiah.

When the people of Judah began to rebuild the temple in Jerusalem, the Samaritans wanted to help but were rejected. With bitterness they turned against the Jews of Jerusalem and proceeded to build their own temple on Mount Gerizim.

The hostility between the Jews and Samaritans was extremely deep-seated and very much alive during Jesus' earthly ministry.

The Samaritans had their own outcasts. The woman in this passage came to draw water at noon, a time when she could avoid contact with the other women of the city. Her reasons? She had been married five times and was now living with a man to whom she was not married. She was, therefore, an outcast of the outcasts. But she was important to Jesus, and he went to Samaria to bring her the good news of the salvation he had come to provide.

Jesus arrests her attention (vv. 7-12)

By speaking to her (vv. 7-9)

No one would have raised an eyebrow about Jesus talking to Nicodemus (a Jew, a man, a religious leader, learned, wealthy, one who recognized Jesus had come from God). Yet here Jesus talks to a Samaritan, which was shocking in and of itself; but she was also a woman, who was an adulteress, ignorant, poor, and with no clue about the identity of the one speaking to her. Isn't it interesting that while Jesus talked to Nicodemus at night, he talked to this woman in broad daylight?

By speaking to her about 'living water' (vv. 10-15)

When this woman came to the well, Jesus approached her in terms of the physical ('Give me a drink'), but he quickly moved to the spiritual ('living water'). It took a while for the woman to realize that Jesus was talking about a different kind of water than that which she could draw (vv. 11-12).

Like this woman, many think exclusively in terms of the here and now. They look upon Christianity as nothing more than another way to help them cope with the challenges of life. They fail to realize their basic need is spiritual in nature and that Christianity deals with that need. Those who stay focused on this life and the needs of the moment will never come to salvation.

> 'Riches, and rank, and place, and power, and learning, and amusements, are utterly unable to fill the soul. He that only drinks of these waters is sure to thirst again'
>
> (J. C. Ryle, *Thoughts*, vol. 1, p.205).

Salvation is appropriately symbolized by water because it cleanses the soul as water cleanses the body. Furthermore, salvation:

* places a new principle within us (v. 14). It is not a matter of merely adding religious activities to our lives. It means an inner transformation has taken place;

* continues throughout this life and finally issues in eternal life (v. 14).

The water of salvation springs unceasingly from a fountain that is placed within. If one truly receives Christ as Lord and Saviour, he will never be able to get away from it. Salvation will always be at work in his life, and when his days on this earth are over he will be ushered into eternal life.

> 'He that has at hand only a bucket of water needs not thirst as long as this lasts, but it will soon be *exhausted*; but believers have in them *a well of water*, overflowing, ever flowing'
>
> (Matthew Henry, vol. v, p.903, italics are his).

Jesus reveals her need for spiritual cleansing (vv. 15-24)

He shows her the reality of sin (vv. 15-18)

The woman had obviously failed to conform to God's commandments. She had gone from husband to husband, totalling five. The implication is that she had violated God's laws on divorce. She was now living with a man who was not her husband, a clear-cut violation of God's demand for sexual morality.

He shows her failure to worship God (vv. 19-24)

Uncomfortable with Jesus' words about her sin, the woman quickly tries to change the subject to one of the most controversial topics of the day — the proper place to worship (v. 20). Those who are faced with their sins often try this!

The woman's strategy only succeeded in opening the door for Jesus to press upon her the reality of her need. Out of aversion toward the Jews, the Samaritans had, without divine sanction, built their own temple upon a site which they had chosen, that is, Mount Gerizim. They had constructed their own religion. The Jewish religion, on the other hand, was based on divine revelation. All who were saved had to embrace through faith the saving truth God had revealed to the Jews.

The controversy between the Samaritans and Jews on the proper place for worship was about to be rendered meaningless because the Messiah to whom the temple and all its rituals pointed had arrived in the person of Jesus. Through the salvation provided by Jesus, God would seek and find people to worship him wholeheartedly with their spirits and according to the truths he has revealed in his Word.

'...the Samaritan religion was a man-made religion, and Jesus would not allow the Samaritan woman to believe that any religion of human origin, a religion based on human ideas is acceptable to Jehovah... Accordingly, salvation was of the Jews alone because only the Jews possessed a religion that had its origin in God. Moreover, it was only in Judaism, with its system of sacrifices and temple worship that there was any true sense of the holiness of God and of the necessity of a substitutionary sacrifice as the grounds of forgiveness and of an acceptable approach to Him'

(James Montgomery Boice, *The Gospel of John*, p.248).

Charles Erdman explains Jesus' reply to her objection:

'He tells the woman that her trouble has not been as to the place of worship, but as to the fact; she has never worshiped at all'

(*John*, p.47).

Jesus reveals himself to her (vv. 25-26)

After Jesus blunted her mention of the controversy on worship, the woman essentially said, 'All of these things are just too difficult for us. We will have to wait until the Messiah comes to sort it all out.' Little did she realize that it was not necessary for her to wait. Jesus identified himself to her in these simple words: 'I who speak to you am he' (v. 26).

'Christ was nearer than she had known! This remains true in the experience of those who come to him in faith today. Believing in him is always a surprising discovery of free grace, unmerited, undeserved and unsought'

(Gordon J. Keddie, vol. 1, pp.187-8).

DIGGING DEEPER

1. *Read verses 1-3. Why did Jesus leave Judea?*

2. *Read verse 4. Why did Jesus need to go to Samaria?*

3. *Read verses 5-9. What does the weariness of Jesus tell us about him? What does his willingness to talk with this woman tell us?*

4. *Read verse 10. What gifts can you identify?*

5. *Read verses 11-14. To what does the phrase 'living water' refer? What do these verses tell us about this water?*

6. *Read verses 15-19. Why did Jesus suddenly change the subject to the woman's husband?*

7. *Read verses 20-26. Why did the woman suddenly change the subject to worship? What constitutes true worship?*

The Samaritan woman is one among many women with whom Jesus had contact during his ministry. Read the following verses. In the blanks provided write the name (or a description) of the woman and what Jesus provided for her:

Jesus and the Samaritan woman   John 4:1-26

                          Woman   Provision

John 8:1-12   _____   _____

John 11:38-40   _____   _____

John 12:3-8   _____   _____

John 19:25-27   _____   _____

John 20:11-18   _____   _____

The spiritual harvest

'Do you not say, "There are still four months and then comes the harvest"? Behold, I say to you, lift up your eyes and look at the fields, for they are already white for harvest!' (4:35).

In these verses, the apostle John describes the sequel to Jesus' conversation with the Samaritan woman. This sequel consists of three parts:

1. The woman tells the people of her village about Jesus;
2. Jesus converses with his disciples;
3. Jesus deals with the Samaritans who came to him after hearing the testimony of the woman.

The one thread that runs through these developments is the truth of spiritual harvest. The first two events can be seen as Jesus sending harvesters. The last event can be seen as Jesus harvesting.

The Lord Jesus sends harvesters (vv. 27,31-38)

Jesus sent the Samaritan woman by converting her (vv. 28-30)

When the woman realized the truth of the things spoken to her by Jesus, she immediately left her waterpot and ran to the village to tell others. The instinctive response of the converted heart is to serve the Lord. The person who says he is saved but has no desire for such service is deceived.

J. C. Ryle forcefully applies the testimony of this woman in this way:

> 'Do we feel the supreme importance of spiritual things, and the comparative nothingness of the things of the world? Do we ever talk to others about God, and Christ, and eternity, and the soul, and heaven, and hell? If not, what is the value of our faith? Where is the reality of our Christianity?'
>
> (*Thoughts*, vol. 1, p.233).

Jesus sent the disciples by instructing them (vv. 27,31-38)

Early in his account of Jesus in Samaria, the apostle John says the disciples had gone into a city to buy food (v. 8). He now makes the point that they returned at the very moment that Jesus concluded his discussion with the Samaritan woman.

William Hendriksen observes:

> '...the divine providence is such that at that exact moment — not earlier, so that the conversation with the woman would have been interrupted; nor later, so that the disciples would have missed this great event (their Lord condescending to a Samaritan woman) with all its missionary implications — the disciples arrived! This is a glorious manifestation and illustration of the operation of God's providence for the furtherance of his kingdom'
>
> (vol. i, p.170).

The disciples, although astonished at the sight of Jesus talking to a woman, studiously avoided saying anything about it. Instead they urged Jesus to eat the food they had purchased (vv. 27,31). Jesus, knowing perfectly their thoughts, used the subject of food to explain that he had been engaged in harvesting a soul for God and to call them to enter the harvest field as well.

1. *Spiritual harvesting is richly rewarding.* Jesus called it his 'meat' (vv. 32,34, AV). Serving the Lord is also meat for us. It gives us the satisfaction of knowing we are doing God's will. It gives us the satisfaction of seeing souls saved through our witness and knowing we are sharing the work with Christ himself and with other Christians (vv. 36-38).

William Hendriksen says:

'Right here in Samaria the Lord had just now commissioned his disciples to reap that for which they had not labored. Others had labored among these Samaritans, and now the disciples have been commissioned to enter into (i.e. to gather the fruits of) their labor... Both Jesus and the Samaritan woman had been laboring among these Samaritans: Jesus indirectly, via the Samaritan woman; she, in turn, directly, among her neighbors. Into this labor the disciples now entered'

(vol. i, pp.174-5).

2. *Spiritual harvesting is urgently needed* (v. 35). The disciples had erected some formidable barriers against doing the work Jesus wanted them to do. They were prejudiced against the Samaritans and they were preoccupied with their own physical needs. Jesus appealed to them to drop these barriers and see the great spiritual harvest that stretched out before them. While the harvest in the physical realm was still four months away, the spiritual harvest was ripe and waiting.

The Lord Jesus continues harvesting (vv. 39-42)

There can be no more heart-warming and encouraging picture than the one portrayed in these verses. Here sinners come to Jesus, and he does not turn them away but welcomes and saves them. Treated as outcasts by the Jews, these despised Samaritans were not beyond the gracious reach of Jesus, the friend of sinners.

> 'Seeing the change in the woman and hearing her story, they determine to try it for themselves. There is a danger of their sins also being exposed, but what does it matter so long as they get the happiness which she has? What does it matter though the whole world may know your past, and all the town laugh at you because of your penitential tears? What does it matter when you know that God has forgiven that past, and you are filled with the joy of salvation and are thrilled with a new life?'
> (D. Martyn Lloyd-Jones, *Evangelistic Sermons*, p.20).

We should note that some of the Samaritans believed in Jesus on the basis of what they heard from the woman (v. 39). Sometimes God creates faith very quickly in human hearts and does so without a full declaration of the truth. Others believed when they came to Jesus and heard him speak for two days (vv. 40-41).

While there are different ways to faith, there is only one faith. That one faith was expressed by the Samaritans. They said they knew that Jesus was 'indeed the Christ, the Saviour of the world' (v. 42).

It is not merely saying these words that makes one a Christian, but rather saying them from a mind that has been convinced and a heart that has embraced the truth about Christ.

DIGGING DEEPER

1. *Read verse 27. Why was it a cause for surprise that Jesus would talk to a woman in public?*

2. *Read verses 28-30. What convinced the woman that Jesus was indeed the Messiah?*

3. *Read verses 31-34. What was Jesus' 'food'? What was the work Jesus had to finish?*

4. *Read verses 35-38. What was the nature of the harvest to which Jesus was referring?*

5. *Read verses 39-42. What caused the Samaritans to believe in Jesus?*

The Samaritans confessed their faith in the Lord Jesus in verse 42. Their words 'we believe' are found in another statement in John's Gospel. Unscramble the following words to find this statement:

yb   hsti   ew   evelieb   htat   ouy   meac   rhoft

____ _____ ____ _____ _____ ____ _____ _____

ofrm   Gdo.

_____ __

Using a concordance, identify the verse in which this statement is found.

_____

Who spoke these words? _____.

Jesus heals the nobleman's son

'Jesus said to him, "Go your way; your son lives."
So the man believed the word that Jesus spoke to
him, and he went his way' (4:50).

The verses of this lesson touch on two aspects of Jesus'
ministry. The first is his move from Samaria to Galilee
(vv. 43-45). The second is his healing of the nobleman's son
(vv. 46-54).

Jesus had been to Galilee before and had been harshly
treated and rejected (Luke 4:18-19). The fact that he now
goes back indicates his determination to do the will of God
and to fulfil the prophecies of the Old Testament (see Matt.
4:13-16) regardless of the consequences.

The healing of the nobleman's son is the second of
the seven signs John presents. It is not difficult for us to
understand why he included it. He wrote his Gospel to
create and sustain faith in Christ, although he knew that all
faith is not true faith, and that there is such a thing as false
faith (2:23-25). He found it necessary, therefore, to frequently
distinguish between the two.

That distinction comes out very clearly in the case of the
nobleman. Very little attention is given to the healing itself.
The focus is not on the nobleman's son, but on the nobleman
and his faith. We can see this man passing through three

distinct phases of faith. Firstly, he obviously believed in the possibility that Jesus could heal his son. Secondly, he believed the word Jesus spoke to him (v. 50); and finally, we are simply told that 'he himself believed' (v. 53), a reference, we may safely assume, to true, saving faith.

The flawed faith with which this man came to Jesus

A temporal faith

John begins his account by reminding us of Jesus' miracle at Cana (v. 46). Jesus was known in this area, then, as a miracle worker. As soon as the nobleman learned Jesus was in Cana, he made the five- or six-hour journey from Capernaum to seek his help.

When he found Jesus he pleaded with him to 'come down' and heal his son (v. 47). Jesus' response indicates that the man's faith in him was as a miracle worker who had come to help people with their temporal, physical problems. There was no understanding that Jesus was the Son of God. Jesus had encountered this same problem before (2:23-25), and his words here should be taken, therefore, as something of a sigh over how little true spiritual discernment he had found.

Jesus was, of course, concerned about the man's temporal problems, but his main concern was much larger, namely, the eternal salvation of this man and his family (Luke 19:10).

The nobleman did not realize that his phrase 'my child dies' would have been true even if the son had not been physically ill at the time. His son, as is true of all, was already sick with sin and doomed to die eternally. How many of us tend to think of our children in terms of their physical needs only and fail to consider their eternal destiny!

'He that is wise will never reckon confidently on long life. We never know what a day may bring forth. The strongest and fairest are often cut down and hurried away in a few hours, while the old and feeble linger on for many years. The only true wisdom is to be always prepared to meet God, to put nothing off which concerns eternity, and to live like men ready to depart at any moment. So living, it matters little whether we die young or old. Joined to the Lord Jesus, we are safe in any event'

> (J. C. Ryle, *Thoughts*, vol. 1, p.255).

A partial, limited faith

The nobleman pleaded with Jesus to come to the place where his son was. He did not understand with whom he was dealing. Jesus did not have to come to the place where the child was, and he did not have to get there before the child died. His power knows no limits.

The features of true faith

It was created by the word of God

The word of God to this nobleman was: 'Go your way; your son lives.' Jesus offered no word of explanation and the nobleman asked for none.

While this word was sounding in his ears, the Spirit of God was working in his heart to cause him to believe. This is a picture of saving faith. It is generated in the heart by the Spirit of God using the Word of God (Rom. 10:17). The sword of the Spirit is the Word of God (Eph. 6:17).

'He that by faith has laid hold on some word of Christ, has got his feet upon a rock. What Christ has said, He is able to do; and what He has undertaken, He will never fail to make good. The sinner who has really reposed his soul on the word of the Lord Jesus, is safe to all eternity. He could not be safer if he saw the Book of Life and his own name written in it'
(J. C. Ryle, vol. 1, p.256).

It brought peace to the heart

The word from Jesus brought assurance to the heart of the nobleman. He spoke to Jesus at 1.00 in the afternoon. While there was still time for him to return to Capernaum before dark, he evidently spent the night in Cana because when he met his servants they referred to 'yesterday' when they spoke of his son's recovery (v. 52). He had such assurance about his son that he did not hasten home.

It accepted Jesus in his fulness

When the servants confirmed that his son's fever had left at the same hour he had spoken to Jesus, the nobleman 'believed'. He realized that Jesus was far more than he had first assumed; he was indeed the Son of God.

It was shared with others

The nobleman himself believed, but all his household believed with him. We should not minimize this. The nobleman was probably an officer of Herod's court. His household would have consisted of far more than his wife and his son. We know from verse 51 that he had servants. The word 'household' includes both family members and servants.

'What an example does this incident furnish us of the mysterious workings of God! — a boy brought to the point of *death* that a whole house might have *eternal life*'
                    (Arthur W. Pink, vol. i, p.238, italics are his).

DIGGING DEEPER

1. *Read verses 43-45. To which feast is John referring?*

2. *Read verses 46-47. What kind of belief did the nobleman have when he came to Jesus?*

3. *Read verse 48. Why was Jesus unhappy with the desire of the people for signs and wonders?*

4. *Read verses 49-50. What kind of belief did the nobleman have at this point?*

5. *Read verses 51-54. What kind of belief did the nobleman have here?*

Use the first letters of the missing words in the verses below to arrive at one of the key words in this week's lesson:

'I will _____ wisely in a perfect way' (Ps. 101:2).

'For the _____ of the Lord run to and fro throughout the whole earth, to show himself strong on behalf of those whose heart is loyal to him' (2 Chron. 16:9).

'The _____ is my shepherd...' (Ps. 23:1).

'His understanding is _____' (Ps. 147:5).

'Therefore, as the _____ of God, holy and beloved, put on tender mercies, kindness, humility, meekness, longsuffering' (Col. 3:12).

'The earth was without form, and _____; and darkness was on the face of the deep' (Gen. 1:2).

'Therefore "if your _____ is hungry, feed him; if he is thirsty, give him a _____"' (Rom. 12:20).

KEY WORD: ___ ___ ___ ___ ___ ___ ___ ___

Jesus heals a lame man

'When Jesus saw him lying there, and knew that he already had been in that condition a long time, he said to him, "Do you want to be made well?"' (5:6).

This passage brings us to the third sign of John's Gospel. Here Jesus heals a man who had been lame for thirty-eight years. This healing took place in Jerusalem where Jesus had gone to attend an unnamed feast (v. 1).

The lame man and the pool (vv. 2-5,7)

The miracle took place at the pool of Bethesda (meaning 'house of outpouring'). This pool, located inside the Sheep Gate of the city, was circled by five 'porches', which were covered colonnades.

The pool was surrounded by 'a great multitude of sick people' (v. 3) who were lying inside the colonnades so that they could have some protection from the weather. They had gathered there because they shared the belief that an angel would come and stir the pool, and the first person who stepped in after the stirring would be healed of his affliction (v. 4).

The fact that the oldest manuscripts of John's Gospel do not contain the last part of verse 3 and all of verse 4 indicates that we are dealing with superstition here rather than with an actual appearance of an angel.

Gordon J. Keddie writes:

'The real issue remains as to whether the text … should be read as a history of what God was doing at Bethesda, or as an account of what people mistakenly attributed to him. That the latter would seem to be the case is confirmed by the fact that Jesus' healing of the man took place apart from the water of the pool. Jesus' true miracle exposed the Bethesda phenomenon for what it was — a grotesque lottery that offered bogus healing to the first and fastest into the water, and so perennially preyed on the desperation of the chronically ill'

(*John*, vol. 1, p.211).

One of this multitude was a man who had been lame for thirty-eight years. The period of his suffering was more than the life span of most of the people of that day.

What causes all the pain and suffering in this world? The Bible tells us that the world is not as God made it. When God created it there was no sickness or death. These things came in as a result of sin. Therefore we should not allow the calamities of life to make us angry at God. We should rather be angry at sin.

'When we read of cases of sickness like this, we should remember how deeply we ought to hate sin! Sin was the original root, and cause, and fountain of every disease in the world. God did not create man to be full of aches, and pains, and infirmities. These things are the fruits of the Fall. There would have been no sickness, if there had been no sin'

(J. C. Ryle, vol. 1, p.267).

We must not forget that this passage, like the one relating to Jesus and the Samaritan woman, intertwines the physical and the spiritual, and the physical situation is used to point to spiritual truth.

The physical condition of this man can be regarded, therefore, as a picture or type of the spiritual condition into which all of us are born. We come into this world spiritually lame, unable to serve God as he intended. The good news is that God, through Christ, makes sinners able to walk in his ways.

Jesus and the lame man (vv. 6,8-9,14)

In the final analysis, our understanding of the nature of this pool is not crucial, and we must not put our focus on it. The truly important point is what Jesus did.

Jesus heals him (vv. 6,8-9)

1. *The perfect knowledge of Jesus.* As Jesus passed by the pool, he came upon this man. There is no indication that he, the lame man, had any knowledge of Jesus or what Jesus had done. But Jesus knew all about him (v. 6). He knew he would be there at the pool, and how very long he had been lame.

2. *The abounding grace of Jesus.* Jesus singled him out of the multitude of sick people and asked if he wanted to be well. This question was necessary because many of the sick and lame of that day made a fairly lucrative living through begging and did not really want to give it up.

> 'Contrary to the Bethesda spring, God's grace is not a spring that flows only intermittently; it is a spring that supplies water constantly. Such grace heals us completely and forever'
> (S. G. DeGraaf, *Promise and Deliverance*, vol. iv, p.45).

3. *The unlimited power of Jesus.* When the man indicated that he did want to be well (v. 7), Jesus simply said, 'Rise, take up your bed and walk' (v. 8). John notes that the man was 'immediately' on his feet and walking (v. 9).

We all come into this world spiritually lame. We are unable to achieve God's purpose for our lives unless something is done to make us spiritually whole. The good news is that the same Lord Jesus Christ who healed this man has spiritually healed all those who have been saved. On the basis of this man's physical healing, we can draw the following conclusions about the Lord granting spiritual healing:

- He knows us as individuals and works with us on that basis (vv. 3,5);
- He always takes the initiative (v. 6);
- He works through our faith in the Word of God (vv. 8-9; Rom. 10:17).

'The miracle certainly attests and encapsulates the very essence of gospel grace. It was sovereignly given, it was attended by the exercise of faith on the part of the recipient and it issued in a radically new life for him'

(Gordon J. Keddie, vol. 1, p.212).

Jesus warns him (v. 14)

While specific sins do sometimes lead to terrible conse-quences, we should not necessarily take Jesus' words to mean that this man had been lame because of a particular sin in his life. The whole world is affected by sin, and we cannot pass through it without being touched by the consequences of sin.

Jesus' warning should rather be taken in a more general way, that is, as a call to this man to repent and believe so that he will not experience catastrophe in eternity — a fate far worse than being crippled in this life!

'...this should be taken as a call to believe and repent, and so escape, in time and eternity, the righteous judgement of God, rather than as connecting the man's particular condition with some specific sin committed thirty-eight years before. It is certainly and universally true that going on sinning will issue in worse things happening in our lives. It is also true that specific sins can have specific and tragic consequences (1 Cor. 11:28-32). There are, however, worse things even than being crippled for a lifetime. There is a lost eternity ahead for the unrepentant!'

(Gordon J. Keddie, vol. 1, pp.215-6).

The healed man and the Jews (vv. 9-13,15)

With the term 'the Jews' (v. 10), John was referring to the religious leaders. Instead of rejoicing over the healing, these men complained that the man was violating the Sabbath by carrying his bed! The truth is that he was doing no such thing. The law only prohibited them from carrying on the Sabbath those burdens that related to business and gain. The problem, then, was not with the healed man but with the religious leaders themselves in that they had distorted the very law they professed to revere.

The healed man responded to their indignant inquiry by saying it was the same man who healed him that told him to carry his bed. At this point he did not know Jesus' name, but he knew that his power to heal meant he also had authority to command.

DIGGING   DEEPER

1. *Read verses 1-4. What details do these verses provide?*

2. *Read verses 5-8. Why did Jesus ask the man if he wanted to be made well? What does this miracle tell us about the Lord Jesus Christ?*

3. *Read verses 9-13. Why were the religious leaders upset about the healing of the man?*

4. *Read verses 14-15. To what does Jesus attribute this man's lameness?*

Read Mark 2:23-28, and answer the following questions:

* What action supposedly violated the Sabbath? _____

_____

* Who raised the accusation? _____
* What example did Jesus use? _____

_____

* What conclusions did Jesus draw? (1) _____

_____ (2)_____.

Jesus responds to the religious leaders

'Most assuredly, I say to you, he who hears my word and believes in him who sent me has everlasting life, and shall not come into judgement, but has passed from death into life' (5:24).

The healing of a man who had been lame for thirty-eight years would seem to be a cause for universal rejoicing, but the religious leaders of the day were enraged because Jesus did it on the Sabbath!

Jesus responded to their fury with these words: 'My Father has been working until now, and I have been working' (v. 17).

When God instituted the Sabbath by resting from his creative work (Gen. 2:2), he did not stop working altogether. He rested only from creating, not from showing concern and compassion for his creation. Jesus' act of healing was, therefore, something of which the Father approved and was, in fact, his own work. In like manner, the Lord's Day (which is the Christian successor to the Sabbath) does not mean the Christian is to do no work at all, but rather he is to turn away from his ordinary work and pleasures to do a different kind of work.

This answer only angered the religious leaders more. They knew Jesus was claiming nothing less than full equality with God. As far as they were concerned, they now had two grounds for killing him — breaking the Sabbath and blaspheming (v. 18).

Jesus claims to be God

Unintimidated by their rage, Jesus refused to withdraw or modify his claim. Instead he confirmed that their conclusion was correct. He was indeed claiming equality with God (vv. 19-20,23,30).

Jesus said this healing was nothing less than God's own work, and that he had done it in dependence upon the Father (v. 19). He also said he could 'do nothing of himself' but only what he saw the Father do (v. 19).

Jesus was not admitting a deficiency and thus contradicting his own claim. He was essentially saying he and the Father were so closely knit together and enjoyed such unity of being that to see one work was to see the other work! In other words, Jesus was saying to these religious leaders: 'When you see me in action, you see God himself in action.'

Any of Jesus' statements that seem to indicate he was inferior to the Father were due to his voluntary submission to the Father in order to work out the plan of redemption. When Jesus took our humanity, he voluntarily adopted a posture of submission to and dependence on the Father. But even as a man he did not cease to be God. He was the God-man — fully God and fully man at one and the same time.

If there were any doubts in the minds of the religious leaders about what Jesus was claiming, he removed them all by making the full affirmation in verse 23, namely, that the Son should be honoured as much as the Father.

Jesus claims to do the works of God

In verse 20 we find Jesus alluding to 'greater works' yet to be done and in verses 21 and 22 he identifies them, adding more details about them in verses 25 to 29. These greater works, granting life and passing judgement, are clearly prerogatives of God. Anyone who can do these things has to be God.

Granting life (vv. 24-26)

1. *Spiritual life for the soul.* The Bible says we are all born with a sinful nature and that sinful nature renders us spiritually dead toward God. We have no interest in God, what he has done, what his Word says, or what his law demands. It is a state of living death — physically alive but spiritually dead!

Praise God, it is not a hopeless state! Jesus has the power to grant spiritual life 'to whom he will' (v. 21). Would you like a picture of this? All you have to do is turn a few pages of John's Gospel and you will find Jesus standing at the tomb of Lazarus. There he cried out, 'Lazarus, come forth!' And out Lazarus came! Carried out by the power of God! (John 11:43-44).

What happened to Lazarus in the physical realm is what has happened to all Christians in the spiritual realm. They were in a spiritual tomb, but one glad day Jesus spoke the word of life to them and they were raised. The apostle Paul says, 'And you he made alive, who were dead in trespasses and sins...' (Eph. 2:1).

2. *Resurrection life for the body* (vv. 25-26). Jesus' power to grant life includes raising the dead. The same God who made the first man from the dust (Gen. 2:7) will have no

trouble reclaiming dead bodies from the dust. While all the dead will be raised (v. 28), they will not all share the same destiny. Some will be raised to eternal life and some to eternal destruction.

Exercising judgement (vv. 27-30)

How is all this determined? The Bible says there is going to be a judge! The apostle Paul says, 'So then each of us shall give account of himself to God' (Rom. 14:12).

This is not just a 2000-year-old religious squabble. Jesus Christ still claims to be God, and that claim has massive significance for every individual. If we are interested in facing death calmly and receiving eternal life, we must be interested in Jesus because he claims authority over these matters. He says he has the power to raise us from the deadness of our sins and to grant us spiritual life (v. 25). He has the power to raise our bodies from the grave, to bring us into judgement (vv. 26-27) and either send us into eternal life or eternal destruction (v. 29).

'The passage is one of those that ought to sink down very deeply into our hearts, and never be forgotten. All is not over when men die. Whether they like it or not, they will have to come forth from their graves at the last day, and to stand at Christ's bar. None can escape His summons. When His voice calls them before Him, all must obey. When men rise again, they will not all rise in the same condition. There will be two classes — two parties — two bodies. Not all will go to heaven. Not all will be saved. Some will rise again to inherit eternal life, but some will rise again only to be condemned. These are terrible things! But the words of Christ are plain and unmistakable. Thus it is written, and thus it must be'

(J. C. Ryle, vol. 1, p.295).

DIGGING   DEEPER

1. *Read verses 16-18. What did the religious leaders want to do with Jesus? Why?*

2. *Read verses 19-23. What are the greater works Jesus promised to do?*

3. *Read verse 21. To whom does the Lord Jesus grant life?*

4. *Read verse 24. What is necessary for a person to have everlasting life?*

5. *Read verses 25-30. What types of resurrection are mentioned here? When will these resurrections occur?*

In the blanks provided write 'C' for each phrase that pertains to the Christian and 'N' for each that pertains to the non-Christian.

_____   Hears my word and believes
_____   Judgement
_____   Everlasting life
_____   Those who have done good
_____   Those who have done evil
_____   Resurrection of condemnation
_____   Resurrection of life
_____   Passed from death to life

WEEK 13

John 5:31-47

Words of evidence and rebuke

 'You search the Scriptures, for in them you think you have eternal life; and these are they which testify of me' (5:39).

The healing of the lame man stirred the hatred of the religious leaders against Jesus. They were first infuriated that Jesus had told this man to carry his bed on the Sabbath day (v. 9). They were further enraged that Jesus claimed to be equal with God (vv. 17-18). Instead of retracting his claim, Jesus proceeded to expand upon it, claiming to have authority to exercise the prerogatives of God (granting life and passing judgement).

The verses before us both continue and conclude John's description of this controversy. Here he reports the evidence Jesus offered for his claims and the rebukes Jesus gave the religious leaders for being unwilling to accept that evidence.

Words of evidence (vv. 31-37,39)

Jesus begins this section by saying, 'If I bear witness of myself, my witness is not true' (v. 31).

He was not saying, of course, that he was speaking falsehood. He was rather acknowledging that which is commonly held, namely, testimony has to be substantiated.

'Our Lord knew that in any disputed question a man's assertions in his own favour are worth little or nothing'

(J. C. Ryle, vol. 1, p.308).

Having acknowledged this principle, the Lord presented his evidence.

The one witness: the Father (vv. 32,37)

The main witness to Jesus was the Father himself. The other witnesses must be considered subordinate to him and even instruments that he employed.

Jesus first speaks of the Father in veiled terms (v. 32) and then explicitly (v. 37). The testimony of the Father to Jesus is not to be identified with those occasions on which the Father spoke from heaven (Matt. 3:17; 17:5). The religious leaders had not heard that testimony. Jesus says they had not 'heard his voice at any time' (v. 37). The Father's testimony is rather to be found in the witnesses Jesus is yet to mention.

The means by which the Father witnessed to Jesus

1. *John the Baptist* (vv. 33-35). John was sent by the Father to bear witness to Jesus, and the religious leaders had heard that witness (John 1:19-34). But instead of believing and accepting it, they turned on John, whom they formerly admired, and rejected Jesus. John was like a shining light, but when the religious leaders did not like what the light revealed, they blew it out!

2. *The works of Jesus* (v. 36). The phrase 'Yet I do not receive testimony from man' means that Jesus did not need to rely entirely on the testimony of John the Baptist. J. C. Ryle says:

> 'Five things should always be noted about our Lord's miracles. (1) Their *number*: they were not a few only, but very many indeed; (2) Their *greatness*: they were not little, but mighty interferences with the ordinary course of nature; (3) Their *publicity*: they were generally not done in a corner, but in open day, and before many witnesses, and often before enemies; (4) Their *character*: they were almost always works of love, mercy, and compassion, helpful and beneficial to man, and not mere barren exhibitions of power; (5) Their *direct appeal to men's senses*: they were visible, and would bear any examination'
>
> (vol. 1, p.311, italics his).

3. *The Scriptures* (v. 39). The religious leaders were in the habit of carefully studying the Scriptures, but with all their searching, they were failing to see what Scripture was about, namely, the Lord Jesus Christ. He was standing before them — the fulfilment of the Old Testament prophecies and types — and they did not recognize him as their Messiah.

Words of rebuke (vv. 38,40-47)

After presenting the evidence for his claims, the Lord Jesus reproves the religious leaders for rejecting the evidence and refusing to believe. He says the following:

* they did not have the Word of God abiding in them (v. 38). While they professed to revere God's Word, they really had no place in their hearts for it;

- they were unwilling to come to Jesus as the Christ and the giver of eternal life (v. 40);

- they did not have the love of God abiding in them (vv. 42-43). They were in the untenable position of claiming to love God on one hand, while denying the very Son whom God loved and sent to them. While they professed love for God, they would willingly embrace someone whom God had not sent (v. 43) instead of embracing the one he had sent;

- they were more concerned about pleasing each other than they were about pleasing God (v. 44);

- they refused to believe the writings of Moses, which they professed to revere the most (vv. 45-47).

DIGGING DEEPER

1. *Read verses 31-32. What do these verses tell us about the nature of God? What reasons do we have for believing that God is the way he is described here?*

2. *Read verses 33-35. What did John the Baptist say of Jesus? Why did the religious leaders turn against John the Baptist?*

3. *Read verse 36. What works of Jesus does John mention in the first five chapters of this Gospel?*

4. *Read verses 37-39. In what ways do the Old Testament Scriptures testify to the Lord Jesus?*

5. *Read verses 40-44. Why are people unwilling to accept the claims of Christ even when those claims are backed by solid evidence?*

6. *Read verses 45-47. Name some verses in which Moses referred to the Lord Jesus.*

From the verses indicated on the right, fill in the blanks with words that begin with the letters indicated on the left.

W_____ (v. 36)

I _____ (vv. 31,32,34,36,41,42,43,45)

T_____ (v. 34)

N_____ (vv. 38,40,41,42,43,44,45,47)

E_____ (v. 39)

S_____ (v. 39)

S_____ (v. 38)

Second Quarter

Jesus feeding five thousand

'And Jesus took the loaves, and when he had given thanks he distributed them to the disciples, and the disciples to those sitting down; and likewise of the fish, as much as they wanted' (6:11).

Jesus performed many miracles, but this is the only one described in all four of the Gospels. It is not hard to see why. Jesus here demonstrated his power and grace to more eyewitnesses than at any other time.

Jesus sees the multitude (vv. 2-5)

The day this miracle took place was one Jesus had set aside to enjoy some solitude with his disciples (Matt. 14:13; Mark 6:30,32; Luke 9:10). The people from the surrounding cities weren't about to tolerate such a thing. The man who had worked so many miracles was right there in their own area and they had to see him for themselves. Jesus was never able to look upon the multitudes with an unfeeling, uncaring heart (Matt. 9:36). So the fact that this particular crowd had interrupted his time of solitude did not prevent him from ministering to them.

Do we feel compassion for the multitudes around us? Or are we, like the priest and Levite in Jesus' parable of the

Good Samaritan (Luke 10:25-37), content to rush right by obvious and crying needs?

Jesus tests Philip (vv. 5-9)

It was late when Jesus finished ministering. The people had not eaten, and the place was so remote that food was not easily attainable. It was at this point that Jesus brought his disciples into the picture. He could have fed this whole multitude without involving the disciples at all. Yet, while Jesus does not need human instruments, he chooses to use them.

Here Jesus made use of Philip, Andrew and a little boy. He first asked Philip where they could buy bread. When Jesus asks a question it is not because he does not know the answer. On this occasion John specifically says Jesus already knew what he was going to do, but he wanted to test Philip. God often presents us with problems and trials so that we can see if we have learned to rely on him or if we are still living on the basis of our own wisdom. We can be sure that when the Lord sends a trial it is to open the door to greater blessing.

Philip failed the test. He calculated that it would take two hundred denarii worth of bread for each person to have 'a little'. Prior to this he had seen Jesus perform miracles (2:1-12; 4:46-54; 5:1-9). That very afternoon he had seen Jesus heal all manner of diseases (Matt. 14:14); but all he could do was come up with 'a little' for each person. How sad to talk about 'a little' in the presence of the one who had demonstrated again and again his power to bless abundantly!

It is easy to see Philip's failure, but it is not easy to see our own. All Christians have, like Philip, been placed in the realm of special grace. We have experienced the Lord's power and know of his ability to bless, but we still have the tendency to subsist on common grace, to live on the same basis as those who do not know the Lord at all. When unbelievers look at us they have the right to expect to see something of supernatural resources, something of special grace, not just the same resources they see in their own lives day after day.

Andrew fared little better than Philip. He brought a boy with his lunch of barley cakes and fish to Jesus, but, like Philip, he was thinking only in little terms: 'What are they among so many?' (v. 9). This was his response even though he was in the presence of one who can not only do the impossible but also delights in doing it through the small, the common and the insignificant.

'The insufficient from the hands of the insignificant became sufficient and significant when placed in the hands of Jesus' (James Montgomery Boice, The Gospel of John, p.382).

Jesus multiplies the loaves and fishes

The focus of this story is Jesus, not the young lad. Jesus took the boy's lunch, gave thanks, broke it in pieces and gave it to the disciples to distribute. As they distributed, the lunch multiplied and everyone had enough to eat! It was the Lord who multiplied the lunch. It was the disciples' hands that simply received it from him and distributed it to the multitude. This provides a picture of what the church is to be doing. As we face the needy multitudes, we must resist the temptation to create a new message but rather give ourselves to faithfully distributing the message we have received from him.

Sometimes we fall into the trap of thinking it all depends on us. Distributing is important work because the Lord has commanded it, but meeting the needs of the multitudes of our age rests finally on his power and grace. Don't forget that this miracle was an act of sheer grace. No one even had the faith to believe that such a multitude could be fed, but Jesus fed it anyway. Thank God that even when our faith fails, his grace does not.

'Let us never doubt for a moment, that the preaching of Christ crucified — the old story of His blood, and righteousness, and substitution — is enough for all the spiritual necessities of all mankind. It is not worn out. It is not obsolete. It has not lost its power. We want nothing new — nothing more broad and kind — nothing more intellectual — nothing more efficacious. We want nothing but the true bread of life, which Christ bestows, distributing faithfully among starving souls. Let men sneer or ridicule as they will: nothing else can do good in this sinful world; no other teaching can fill hungry consciences, and give them peace. We are all in a wilderness. We must feed on Christ crucified, and the atonement made by His death, or we shall die in our sins'

(J. C. Ryle, *Thoughts*, vol. 1, p.329).

Jesus resists the king-makers (vv. 4,14-15)

Since it was the Passover (v. 4), it was inevitable that the people would think of Moses leading their fathers from Egypt into the wilderness where they were sustained with bread from heaven. Moses had promised that God would give Israel another Moses-like prophet (Deut. 18:15). Suddenly everything began to click. They were in the wilderness, and they had been fed with bread from another miracle-worker. Jesus must be the prophet Moses promised!

They were correct. Jesus was indeed the promised prophet. But from that correct conclusion they jumped to one that was entirely false. They thought all that was necessary was for them to proclaim Jesus as their king and he would lead them in victorious rebellion against Rome and set up a cradle-to-grave society where all their material needs would be met.

They did not realize that Jesus' kingdom was completely different from what they imagined. It was not temporal and material in nature but spiritual, one that is set up in the hearts of his followers. And it will not come into final and full expression until after this world is finished.

This self-seeking crowd essentially wanted to dictate to Jesus the kind of king he should be, instead of accepting the kingdom he came to offer. When they realized on the very next day that Jesus would never bend to their desires they turned their backs and walked away (6:59-66).

Many today are much like the multitude. Instead of following God's demands, they insist that he yield to theirs. Some carry this to ridiculous lengths. Upon hearing what the Bible says about God's nature, one young lady responded: 'If he is like that, I just won't believe in him any more.'

How is it with us? Do we want Jesus on his terms or on ours? Are we willing to bow before him as he is or do we insist on trying to change him into a Christ with whom we can be comfortable? May God help us to realize that the only Christ who can meet our deepest needs and longings is the one revealed in Holy Scripture.

DIGGING DEEPER

1. *Read verses 1-3. What information do these verses give us regarding the ministry of Jesus?*

2. *Read verse 4. Why do you think John mentions the Passover at this point?*

3. *Read verse 5. What does this verse teach us about the disposition of Jesus?*

4. *Read verses 6-9. What do these verses tell us about Philip and Andrew?*

5. *Read verses 10-13. What conclusions do these verses enable us to draw about Jesus?*

6. *Read verses 14-15. What did the people want to do with Jesus? Why?*

Across:
2. The time at which Jesus fed the 5000.
3. Part of what the lad gave to Jesus
4. 'This is truly the...'

Jesus feeding five thousand   John 6:1-15

Down:

1. The brother of Simon Peter
2. The disciple who calculated the cost
5. The number of baskets of fragments

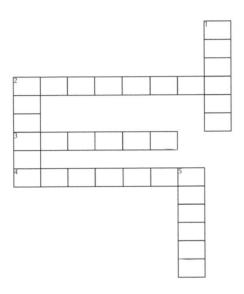

WEEK 15
John 6:15-21

Jesus and the storm

'But he said to them, "It is I; do not be afraid."' (6:20).

The coming of Jesus to his disciples in a terrible storm is the fifth of the seven signs in John's Gospel. To correctly understand it, we must remember the following:

1. It is connected with the feeding of the five thousand;
2. It was performed in the presence of no one except Jesus' disciples.

The miraculous feeding evidently did something to the disciples that made this particular sign necessary. John says it caused the multitude to want to make Jesus king (v. 15).

Jesus knew his disciples were easy prey for the emotion of that moment. Sharing the belief of the crowd that the Messiah's kingdom would be material and political, they would have been eager for Jesus to do as the crowd wanted, that is, declare himself king, lead the people in triumph to Jerusalem, throw off Roman rule and restore Israel to pre-eminence.

Jesus rose to the challenge by doing three things. Firstly, he ordered the disciples to get into their boat and row to the other side of the lake. John simply says, 'His disciples went down to the sea' (v. 16). Matthew and Mark tell us that Jesus 'made' them do this (Matt. 14:22; Mark 6:45). In so doing, Jesus was preventing them from becoming caught up with the crowd's mistaken notion of kingship. Secondly, he sent the multitude away (Mark 6:45). How does one just dismiss a multitude that is caught in a fever pitch of excitement? It was no problem for Jesus. His majestic, authoritative word was more than sufficient for the task. Thirdly, Jesus himself retired to seek the Father's face in prayer (Mark 6:46). Here he faced again the temptation Satan used in the wilderness, namely, to bypass the cross and seize the crown. But the temptation was even stronger now. In the wilderness, one voice whispered enchantingly. Here five thousand thundered it passionately.

An hour or two was all that would normally have been necessary for the disciples to cross the Sea of Tiberias, but this would be no normal crossing. They hadn't rowed very long before they ran into a ferocious storm.

Jesus sent the storm

John has shown again and again that Jesus had divine knowledge (2:24; 4:17-18). Can there be any doubt that he knew the storm was coming? After the storm was over, we do not find him saying, 'Hey fellows, I'm sorry. If I had known a storm was brewing I wouldn't have sent you out.'

Jesus knew the storm was coming because he ordered it to come! The storm came by his design! It wasn't a matter of him failing to check Galilee's weather forecast.

Why would Jesus do this? Didn't he love his disciples? It was precisely because of that love that he sent the storm. He wanted to teach them in an unforgettable way the nature of his kingship. The crowd had it all wrong. His kingdom was not designed to bring his followers ease and comfort. The storm showed them that he had called them away from a life of ease to a life of hardship and difficulty (Phil. 1:29; 2 Tim. 3:12; 1 Peter 4:12).

> 'The walking on the water is a miracle which offers a striking contrast to the conception of Jesus which the multitudes had shown. It reveals, not a political leader, with power in a restricted, earthly sphere, but a divine Creator who has supreme authority in the universe'
>
> (Charles R. Erdman, *John*, p.61).

Jesus shared the storm

Jesus finally came to the disciples in the midst of the storm, but only after several hours. Can we say then that Jesus shared the storm? Mark's Gospel says Jesus saw them struggling as he was praying (Mark 6:48). Jesus shared in their struggle even though they did not realize it. We sometimes wonder if the Lord knows and cares about our difficulties. We can rest assured that he does. When he seems to have withdrawn from us, he sees us and cares about us.

> 'While the storm was raging, and the darkness enveloped the little group of men, they were, nevertheless, perfectly safe, for upon the hill the Lord was interceding for them. A beautiful picture, indeed, one which has many present-day applications'
>
> (William Hendriksen, *John*, vol. i, p.225).

When Jesus walked towards them, the disciples thought they were seeing a ghost. They weren't expecting to see Jesus

111

walking on the water! Although they had seen miracles that very day, they weren't ready for this. Their faith was weak and their hearts were hard (Mark 6:52). How often we fail to see Jesus in the midst of our trials! He draws nigh to us in his Word to speak promises of comfort and strength, but we are so absorbed with the trials that we do not hear his voice.

It is wonderful to know that Jesus is concerned enough about our difficult situations to come in and share them with us, but that only makes the storm more bearable. It does not keep it from raging.

'So is Christ ever with his followers in the midnight and the storm. Thus can he cheer and save'
(Charles R. Erdman, *John*, p.62).

Jesus stopped the storm

There were really two storms raging that night: the one that tossed the ship and caused the disciples to strain their bodies and the one that tossed their hearts and strained their faith. When Jesus stilled the storm raging around their boat he also stilled the storm in their hearts.

The disciples must have had heavy hearts as they climbed into that boat. Was Jesus really the Messiah? How could he do miracles if he was not? But if he was the Messiah why was he so reluctant to claim his throne? If the people were on his side, what could be gained by waiting? By calming the storm Jesus was saying in effect: 'Just because I have refused to be king because I was able to multiply the bread does not mean I am not a king at all. I will be king on my terms, not on the basis of what is popular.' The message got through to the disciples. John says they willingly received him into the boat. Matthew says they fell down and worshipped him (Matt. 14:33). There could be no doubt about whether he was the Messiah. Anyone who has the wind and waves at his beck and call has to be king!

Has the message got through to us? Jesus Christ is King of Kings and Lord of Lords! The test of whether we understand this is whether we worship him. Anyone who really believes that Jesus is king cannot help but worship. Anyone who refuses to do so only shows that he does not really believe Jesus is king.

DIGGING DEEPER

1. Read verses 15-19. What details do these verses provide about the disciples' circumstances?

2. Read verses 20-21. How did Jesus comfort the disciples? What was their response?

After reading the parallel accounts in Matthew 14:22-33 and Mark 6:45-52, write 'T' beside the statements that are true and 'F' beside those that are false.

_____   The stilling of the storm is one of seven signs in John's Gospel.

_____ Jesus could not see the disciples in the storm.

_____ Jesus commanded Simon Peter to walk on the water.

_____ Simon succeeded at first and then began to sink.

_____ Jesus commended Simon for his great faith.

_____ Jesus and the disciples reached land after several more hours of rowing.

Jesus and the miracle-seekers

'Do not labour for the food which perishes, but for the food which endures to everlasting life, which the Son of Man will give you, because God the Father has set his seal on him' (6:27).

As the people walked away from their meal of fish and bread, they took note of the fact that the disciples had taken the only boat available, leaving Jesus behind. Tomorrow would be another day. Although Jesus did not want to be king today, he might change his mind. If he did not, they could at least count on him to provide them with another meal. The crowd left, then, with the next day very much on their minds. Having seen Jesus stay behind, they felt sure they would have no trouble locating him.

When the day dawned, Jesus was nowhere to be found. He must have joined his disciples on the other side of the lake. But how could he have done so when there was only one boat? Many decided that they would cross the lake and look for him in Capernaum. There they made their way to the synagogue and found Jesus teaching (v. 59). When he finished they asked: 'Rabbi, when did you come here?' (v. 25). If he had crossed the night before when no boats were available, another miracle had taken place!

Jesus did not answer their question. He was not interested in people who just wanted to see him perform miracles. The miracles were merely signs; they were not intended to call attention to themselves but to the power and glory of the one who performed them. The miracles were designed to put the true identity of Jesus at the centre of the thinking of these people, but they held that spot for their own comfort.

Jesus rebukes the people (vv. 26-29)

Jesus responded to their inquiry about his arrival in Capernaum by reproving them for being concerned only about the miracles (v. 26) and by urging them to seek the right kind of 'food' (v. 27).

In other words, he distinguishes between the food that perishes and the food that endures. The former refers to temporal things, the latter to spiritual things. How many devote their time and energy to seeking those things that will soon perish! How few devote sufficient attention to seeking those things that will finally issue into eternal life!

> 'The things of the world are *meat that perishes*. Worldly wealth, honour, and pleasure, are *meat*; they *feed the fancy* (and many times this is all) and *fill the belly*. These are things which men *hunger* after as *meat*, and glut themselves with … but they *perish*, are of a perishing nature, wither of themselves, and are exposed to a thousand accidents; those that have the largest share of them are not sure to have them while they live, but are sure to leave them and lose them when they die'
>
> (Matthew Henry, vol. v, p.945, italics are his).

How can we get this spiritual food that leads to eternal life? We must work for it! And what kind of work are we to do?

Jesus' answer is plain: 'This is the work of God, that you believe in him whom he sent' (v. 29).

When it comes to salvation, our work is to do *no* work, but rather to rest on the work of Christ.

Jesus made it clear that he was not speaking about these matters as someone who merely had an opinion to contribute. He was speaking with special authority, as the one who had been validated and confirmed by God the Father (v. 27).

The people call for a sign (vv. 30-34)

At this point the people are beginning to feel uneasy with what Jesus is saying. They sense that he is taking them in a direction they do not want to go. He has rebuked them for their interest in temporal things. He has claimed to have the seal of God affixed to himself. He has called them to believe in him as their spiritual king. These are such disconcerting things that these people want to know by what right Jesus speaks in this way. They want him to perform a sign — as if the one the day before were not sufficient! (v. 30).

Furthermore, they remind him that he was not yet on a par with Moses who had fed their fathers in the wilderness with bread from heaven. Moses did not start with loaves and fish as Jesus had. And Moses did his miraculous feeding for forty years, not just once as Jesus had. And Moses did it for several hundred thousand, not just five thousand!

How fickle these people were! The day before, they were ready to make Jesus king! Now they are ready to turn against him.

Many today are much like them. As long as religion says what they want to hear and talks about meeting their needs, they are for it; but when it begins to cut, they turn away.

Jesus identifies himself as the bread of life
(vv. 35-40)

What he, as bread, provides (v. 35)

We all intuitively feel that we must stand before God and give account of ourselves. We feel guilty about our lives and uncertain about the future. When we believe in Jesus, we are satisfied regarding these matters. There is no need to feel guilty about our sins because Jesus has paid for them. There is no need to feel uncertain about the future because Jesus has guaranteed it to be glorious for his people.

> 'Our bodies could better live without food than our souls without Christ'
>
> (Matthew Henry, vol. v, p.948).

How this bread is appropriated (vv. 35-36)

The words 'come' and 'believe' (v. 35) are synonymous. To come to Jesus is to believe in him. To believe in him is to come to him. If we are to have the spiritual bread we need, we must come to the Lord Jesus Christ, depending on him and him alone for salvation. The religious leaders to whom Jesus was speaking at this point had refused to do this (v. 36).

A promise for those who come and believe (vv. 37-40)

Jesus promises that he will not 'cast out' or turn away anyone who truly comes to him (v. 37), and every person the Father has given to Christ will definitely come to him.

'The eternal purpose of the Almighty cannot fail; the sovereign will of the Lord Most High cannot be frustrated. All, every one, that the Father gave to the Son before the foundation of the world "shall come to him". The Devil himself cannot keep one of them away'

(Arthur W. Pink, vol. i, pp.329-30).

'How welcome should this word be to our souls which bids us welcome to Christ! ... The duty required is a pure gospel duty: *to come to Christ,* that we may come to God by him ... The promise is a pure gospel promise: *I will in no wise cast out —* ... We have reason to fear that he should *cast us out.* Considering our meanness, our vileness, our unworthiness to come, our weakness in coming, we may justly expect that he should frown upon us, and shut his doors against us; but he obviates these fears with this assurance...'

(Matthew Henry, vol. v, p.952, italics are his).

Furthermore, he will 'lose nothing' (v. 39). All who come to him in faith in this life will be preserved by him and safely brought home to eternal glory.

'In these and many other passages Scripture teaches a counsel that cannot be changed, a calling that cannot be revoked, an inheritance that cannot be defiled, a foundation that cannot be shaken; a seal that cannot be broken, and a life that cannot perish'

(William Hendriksen, vol. i, p.235).

DIGGING DEEPER

1. *Read verses 22-25. Why were the people so interested in the whereabouts of Jesus?*

2. *Read verses 26-27. What kind of food does Jesus offer?*

3. *Read verses 28-29. What does it mean to do 'the work of God'?*

4. *Read verses 30-34. What kind of bread were the people looking for?*

5. *Read verses 35-40. What promises does Jesus make in these verses?*

'I am the bread of life' (vv. 35,41,48) is the first of the 'I am' sayings in John's Gospel. Look up the Scripture references shown below and write the other sayings in the blanks provided.

8:12   _____

10:9   _____

10:11,14 _____

11:25   _____

14:6   _____

15:1,5   _____

WEEK 17
John 6:41-59

Jesus and the religious leaders

 'I am the living bread which came down from heaven. If anyone eats of this bread, he will live for ever; and the bread that I shall give is my flesh, which I shall give for the life of the world' (6:51).

After feeding the 5000, Jesus miraculously crossed the Sea of Galilee to Capernaum. The next day some of the 5000 found him there teaching in the synagogue (v. 59). After rebuking them for being exclusively concerned about temporal bread (vv. 26-27), Jesus identified himself as the spiritual bread from heaven that truly satisfies (vv. 35-40).

The religious leaders, whom John consistently identifies with the term 'the Jews', complained about Jesus calling himself bread from heaven (v. 41). The verses above contain Jesus' conversation with these religious leaders.

Jesus explains their unwillingness to believe (vv. 41-47)

The religious leaders found themselves in a quandary over Jesus' claim to be bread from heaven (vv. 32-33). They knew his background. Joseph was his father; Mary was his mother. Nazareth was his home town. How could he claim to be from heaven?

It never occurred to them that there could be more to Jesus than these things, which itself was evidence of one of Christianity's central doctrines: that left to ourselves, we are incapable of understanding and receiving spiritual things! (1 Cor. 2:14).

Jesus made this point abundantly plain in these words: 'No one can come to me unless the Father who sent me draws him...' (v. 44).

> 'Salvation is most exactly suited to the sinner's needs, but it is not at all suited to his natural inclinations. The Gospel is too spiritual for his carnal mind: too humbling for his pride: too exacting for his rebellious will: too lofty for his darkened understanding: too holy for his earthbound desires'
>
> (Arthur W. Pink, vol. i, p.336).

The good news is that God draws! He draws sinners to himself by enlightening their minds so that they can understand the truth of God, by enlivening their affections so that they love that truth and by energizing their wills so they can repent and believe. This work of drawing should have come as no surprise to these men because it was proclaimed by the prophets (v. 45).

How do we know whether God is drawing us? If we will come to God with true belief, we can be sure his drawing has taken place in us (v. 47). We must not make the mistake of concerning ourselves about his business. We must rather be occupied with coming to God!

> 'Believing is *not* the cause of a sinner obtaining Divine life, rather is it the *effect* of it. The fact that a man believes, is the evidence that he *already* has Divine life within him'
>
> (Arthur W. Pink, vol. i, p.340).

Jesus repeats and enlarges his claim
(vv. 48-51)

The opposition of the religious leaders did not cause Jesus to retract or modify what he had said. He told the people who had followed him to Capernaum that he was the bread of life (v. 35). He now says it again for the benefit of the religious leaders (v. 48).

In claiming to be bread from heaven, Jesus was asserting something that seemed to the religious leaders to be extremely arrogant and audacious, namely, that he, Jesus, was far superior to Moses. Their fathers ate bread from heaven when Moses was their leader. But that was physical bread which could not even sustain physical life. They ate it, but they still had to die (v. 49). Jesus was offering spiritual bread. Those who ate it would live for ever (vv. 50-51).

How could Jesus claim to be spiritual bread that gives eternal life? He supplies the answer in these words: '...the bread that I shall give is my flesh, which I shall give for the life of the world' (v. 51).

In other words, Jesus is the bread that gives eternal life by virtue of his death on the cross. Why do we not have spiritual and eternal life by nature? To put it another way, why are we spiritually dead? And the answer, of course, is sin, which separates us from God, makes us spiritually dead towards him and places us under the sentence of his wrath.

The cross was designed to deal with all of this. On the cross, Jesus bore the sins of his people and took the wrath of God in their stead. Because Jesus received the penalty for them, there is nothing left for them to pay. Through him the sentence of eternal death is lifted, and they are given eternal life.

Jesus explains how he, as bread, is appropriated (vv. 52-59)

He tells these religious leaders that they must eat his flesh and drink his blood (vv. 53-54). What was he saying? The answer is plain when we lay verse 47 alongside verse 54. In the former, Jesus says, 'he who believes in me has everlasting life'. In the latter, he says, 'Whoever eats my flesh and drinks my blood has eternal life...'

The only difference in these verses is that verse 47 requires believing while verse 54 requires eating and drinking. It should be obvious that the two are one and the same. To 'eat Jesus' flesh and drink his blood' is to believe in his atoning death. As we appropriate physical food to our bodies by eating it, we appropriate Jesus' death to our souls by believing in him as our Lord and Saviour.

The fact that Jesus came into this world does not automatically save us any more than a bread truck passing by puts bread on our tables. As we have to personally get the bread from the truck and eat it, so we must personally receive spiritual bread from Jesus by believing in him. But even the believing is something for which we cannot take credit. We believe because God gave us to his Son in eternity past (v. 37) and because God draws us to Christ (v. 44).

DIGGING DEEPER

1. Read verses 41-42. Why did the religious leaders complain about Jesus?

2. *Read verses 43-45. How did Jesus explain the unwillingness of the religious leaders to believe?*

3. *Read verse 46. What is Jesus claiming here?*

4. *Read verses 48-51,57-58. What is the difference between the manna God gave through Moses and the bread the Lord Jesus was offering?*

5. *Read verses 47,52-56. How do we receive the Lord Jesus Christ?*

Use the first letters of the missing words in the verses below to arrive at a key phrase in this lesson:

'who himself bore our sins in his own _____ on the tree...' (1 Peter 2:24).

'_____ in the Lord always' (Phil. 4:4).

'He who has an _____ , let him hear what the Spirit says to the churches' (Rev. 2:7).

'I have set the LORD _____ before me...' (Ps. 16:8).

'And the _____ in Christ will rise first' (1 Thess. 4:16),

'The Lord GOD has _____ my ear...' (Isa. 50:5).

'Catch us the _____...' (Song of Sol. 2:15).

'...and _____ , I am with you always...' (Matt. 28:20).

'___ will teach you the _____ of the LORD' (Ps. 34:11).

'Keep your tongue from _____...' (Ps. 34:13).

KEY PHRASE: ___ ___ ___ ___ ___ ___ ___ ___ ___ ___ ___

Discipleship tested by doctrine

'But Simon Peter answered him, "Lord, to whom shall we go? You have the words of eternal life"' (6:68).

This passage brings two more groups to our attention. We have already met the multitude — those who had been miraculously fed by Jesus and who wanted him to continue to meet their physical needs. These people were content to live on the physical or material level and seldom allowed their thoughts to rise to higher things.

Then there were the religious leaders whom John calls 'the Jews'. These were the men who had gathered in the synagogue to hear Jesus teach. When the multitude entered the synagogue and engaged Jesus in conversation, these men listened for a while, but then became outraged at what he said and joined the conversation.

In this passage we meet those whom John calls 'disciples', and we are surprised to read that they turned from Jesus (v. 66). These disciples are carefully distinguished from 'the twelve' who stayed with Jesus (v. 67).

These four groups are still with us. Two of them are outside the church and two inside. Firstly, there are those who, like the multitude, live for the moment and give little thought to spiritual matters. There are also those who, like the religious leaders, are antagonistic to Christianity. The church herself is made up of two groups. The first of these consists of those who, like the disciples, have been attracted to Jesus and have begun following him only to lose interest. Then there are those who never openly depart from Christ but continue to follow him. But in this group there are two types, those represented by Simon Peter and those represented by Judas Iscariot. In other words, among those who outwardly stay true to Jesus there are those who truly belong to him and those who appear to belong but do not.

This lesson focuses our attention on the 'disciples' and the 'twelve'.

The disciples who turned away (vv. 60-66)

The reason

How long these people had been following Jesus is impossible to say. It may have been for only a few hours and almost certainly no more than a few days. Jesus had been to Capernaum before and his previous visits may have caused them to consider themselves his disciples. When he returned, they eagerly went to the synagogue to hear him.

As they listened to Jesus dialogue with the remnant of the multitude and the religious leaders, their delight began to vanish. He was saying things they never expected. They began to whisper their shock and displeasure to each other: 'This is a hard saying; who can understand it?' (v. 60).

What had Jesus said? Firstly, he stressed that he was the bread of God that had come down from heaven. God had given him a body and he was now God in human flesh and was, therefore, invested with divine authority. Secondly, he emphasized the absolute necessity of him having to give up his body in death. Thirdly, in alleging that his body had to be 'eaten', even as the priests ate of the flesh of the animals they sacrificed, he was declaring himself to be the fulfilment of those sacrifices. Fourthly, he underscored the vital requirement that each individual should believe in him and his work as the only hope for eternal salvation. Finally, he stressed the terrible damage that sin had done — damage so great and so extensive that apart from the grace of God no one can come to him as Lord and Saviour.

These teachings are the essential core of Christianity, and, sadly enough, many still find them offensive.

The response of Jesus (vv. 61-65)

a. He offered them a word of *confirmation* by pointing them to his coming ascension, which would prove his teachings (v. 62). They would have less trouble believing he came from heaven if they would stay with him long enough to see him return there.

b. He offered a word of *clarification*. He was not calling them to eat his flesh and drink his blood in a physical, literal way, but rather was asking them to believe his word (v. 63). His flesh could not in and of itself help them spiritually. It is his word, which is also the word of the Spirit of God, that produces life. That word creates faith, and faith applies that word to our souls even as eating and drinking apply food and water to our bodies.

c. He offered a word of *confrontation* (vv. 64-65). The problem with those to whom Jesus was speaking was their unwillingness to believe in Jesus' life-giving words. The fact that Jesus knew who did not believe and who would betray him (v. 65) was additional proof that he was God in human flesh.

'It is not for lack of evidence that people reject Jesus Christ. It takes more than schooling to make a Christian. It takes a work of God's sovereign grace'

(Gordon J. Keddie, *John*, vol. 1, p.276).

The twelve who stayed (vv. 67-71)

As the crowd melted away, Jesus turned to the twelve and asked: 'Do you also want to go away?' Simon Peter, as he so often did, spoke for the whole group. His words and Jesus' response to them are filled with meaning.

* Simon's confession shows what is truly important — eternal life. If something is out there awaiting us, something beyond the grave that lasts for ever, we are exceedingly foolish to not prepare for it (Matt. 16:26).

* Simon's confession tells us where eternal life can be found — in the words of the Lord Jesus.

* Simon's confession tells that eternal life can be found in Jesus alone ('Lord, to whom shall we go?' — v. 68).

* Jesus' response tells us that it is possible to be deceived about whether we have eternal life (vv. 70-71).

Here were twelve disciples. All seemed to share the sentiment of Simon Peter. But Jesus knew all men perfectly. He knew that there among the twelve was a hypocrite. This should be a consolation to us, that if this was true of one of those closest to Jesus, we can rest assured it is going to be true today.

DIGGING DEEPER

1. *Read verse 60. What does this verse tell us about human nature?*

2. *Read verse 61. What does this verse teach us about the disposition of Jesus?*

3. *Read verses 62-63. What proof does Jesus offer for the validity of his message?*

4. *Read verses 64-65. What do these verses teach us about sinful human nature?*

5. *Read verses 66-69. Why did Simon Peter and the other disciples stay with Jesus?*

6. *Read verses 70-71. What do these verses tell us about Jesus?*

Unscramble the following words to find a line from an Old Testament confession that is similar to Simon's:

Ttenear   em otn ot vaeel uyo ro ot ntru

_____ ___ ___ __ _____ ____ __ __ _____

ckba   mrof   wlongfoil   ferat   yuo

____ _____ _____ _____ ____

Use a concordance to find the verse of Scripture in which
these words are found _____. Who spoke these
words? _____.

The Feast of Tabernacles

'If anyone wills to do his will, he shall know concerning the doctrine, whether it is from God or whether I speak on my own authority' (7:17).

The Feast of Tabernacles was an annual celebration in Jerusalem that lasted for a period of eight days. During this time the people lived in temporary booths, as a reminder of their fathers who dwelt in temporary shelters during their wilderness years.

Before the feast (vv. 1-10)

Before leaving for the feast, Jesus received unsolicited advice from his brothers — who had not accepted him as the Messiah (v. 5) — regarding the proper conduct of his ministry. They could have been motivated to some degree by family loyalty ('We don't believe he is the Messiah, but he does. So it's our duty to help him out').

But their primary motive appears to have been pity, brought on by the fact that the gigantic crowds had turned away (6:66-67). With this in view, his brothers may have said: 'The poor guy thinks he is the Messiah, but he doesn't have a clue as to how to go about it. He must stop trying to win a following among these country folk in Galilee and sell himself in Jerusalem.'

Whatever their motive, their advice was not sound. Twice in his response, Jesus refers to his 'time' (vv. 6,8). The Gospel of John refers several times to the 'hour' of Jesus (2:4; 7:30; 8:20; 12:23,27-28; 13:1; 17:1). In each case, the word 'hour' translates the Greek word *'hora'* and refers to his death on the cross. But the word Jesus uses with his brothers is *'kairos'*, which refers to the right moment or the right opportunity for doing something.

This tells us that Jesus was wholly aware that his life was following a definite timetable or schedule. His brothers could think in terms of the pragmatic, desirable and convenient (v. 6), but he had to govern his life in terms of the mission the Father had assigned him. His brothers could think and act on the terms of the world because they were at peace with it. But Jesus was not at peace with the world because he told the truth about it, namely, that it was evil (v. 7).

At the feast (vv. 11-24)

The debate about Jesus (vv. 11-13)

Before Jesus even appeared at the feast, there was much discussion about him among the people. John uses the word 'murmuring' — 'quiet debate, whisper, or dispute' — to summarize it. He also simply says 'the people' were engaged in this debate. This is probably a reference to those who had gathered in Jerusalem for the feast. When these people arrived in Jerusalem they found that Jesus was the 'hot topic' of conversation. He had greatly upset the religious leaders on his last visit to Jerusalem by healing a lame man on the Sabbath and by claiming to be equal with God (John 5).

We can be sure that news of Jesus had circulated throughout the whole nation of Israel. So when these people came to Jerusalem for the feast and started hearing what Jesus had done there, they quickly entered the fray. They appear to have discussed only two options: Jesus was either a good man, or he was a deceiver. He was, of course, a good man, but he was much more than that, namely, the God-man.

Debate still swirls around the person of Jesus, and it still follows the same general lines. Some think of him as a good man, a good teacher, a great moral and ethical leader. Others believe he was a fraud, and wonder how there could still be so much fascination with him. The only adequate explanation for Jesus is the same today as it was then — he was God in human flesh.

The teaching of Jesus (vv. 14-24)

In the middle of the feast, Jesus went to the temple to teach (v. 14). The religious leaders were astounded. How could he teach in this way without having studied in any of the rabbinical schools? (v. 15). Jesus responded to their amazement by affirming three things about his teaching:

- it came from God (v. 16);
- it was self-validating (v. 17);
- it glorified God (v. 18).

Joseph Hall offers this paraphrase for verse 17:

> 'If any man shall, with a simple and honest heart, yield himself over to do the will of my Father, according to the measure of that he knows, God shall encourage and bless that man with further light; so as he shall fully know whether my doctrine be of God, or of myself'
>
> (cited by J. C. Ryle, *Thoughts*, vol. 2, p.23).

J. C. Ryle explains verse 17 in this way:

'The principle here laid down is one of immense importance. We are taught that clear knowledge depends greatly on honest obedience, and that distinct views of Divine truth cannot be expected, unless we try to practise such things as we know. Living up to our light we shall have more light. Striving to do the few things we know, we shall find the eyes of our understanding enlightened, and shall know more'

(vol. 2, p.22).

DIGGING DEEPER

1. *Read verses 1-4. What did Jesus' brothers advise him to do? Why did they offer this advice?*

2. *Read verses 5-9. Why did Jesus respond to their advice as he did?*

3. *Read verse 7. Why did the world hate Jesus?*

4. *Read verses 10-13. What two groups of people does John designate in these verses?*

5. *Read verses 14-19. What do these verses tell us about the teaching of Jesus?*

6. *Read verses 20-24. How did Jesus defend his healing of the lame man (John 5:1-8)?*

Find in the following verses of Scripture the words to complete the statements that J. C. Ryle made about Jesus' brothers:

'The mere _____ [Ps. 2:8] of _____ [Gal. 6:1] privileges never yet made any one a Christian. All is useless without the _____ [James 5:16, AV] and applying _____ [Ps. 8:3] of God the Holy Ghost'
(J. C. Ryle, vol, 2, p.2).

The Feast of Tabernacles concluded

'He who believes in me, as the Scripture has said, out of his heart will flow rivers of living water' (7:38).

With these verses the apostle John concludes his account of Jesus attending the Feast of Tabernacles in Jerusalem. These verses fall quite naturally into three major divisions.

The ongoing debate about Jesus (vv. 25-36)

Among the inhabitants of Jerusalem (vv. 25-31)

Confusion reigned among these people. Knowing the religious leaders were seeking to kill Jesus, they marvelled at his boldness (vv. 25-26) and wondered if the leaders had come to the conclusion that he was indeed the Messiah (v. 26). But they quickly dismissed this idea, because they subscribed to one of the popular notions of the day, namely, that no one would know where the Messiah was from (v. 27). Knowing Jesus was from Nazareth, they concluded that he could not be the Messiah.

Jesus responded to their confusion by clearly claiming to be, not from Nazareth, but from God (vv. 28-29). Some were enraged by this (v. 30), but others believed in him (v. 31).

Among the religious leaders (vv. 32-36)

The uproar among the people gave the leaders a pretext for sending officers to arrest Jesus (v. 32). The debate about Jesus intensified when he said he would be with them only a short while before returning to the one who sent him, that is, to the Father (vv. 32-36). His return to the Father would furnish decisive and dramatic proofs of all his claims.

The gracious invitation of Jesus (vv. 37-39)

The Feast of Tabernacles included a water-pouring ceremony each day to commemorate God's miraculous provision of water in the wilderness (Exod. 17:6; Num. 20:11). On each of the seven feast days water was drawn with a golden pitcher from the pool of Siloam and carried in a grand procession to the temple. On the last day of the feast, 'that great day of the feast', there were seven processions instead of one.

Jesus used this ceremony to call the people to the living water of salvation that he alone can supply.

An extensive appeal: 'if anyone thirsts'

People have been known to complain about being slighted. Perhaps they were not invited to a party they wanted to attend. The Lord Jesus does not slight anyone here. All are invited to come and receive the satisfaction he offers. God is so earnest about this matter of including all that he repeats his invitation again and again (Isa. 1:18; 55:1-3; Matt. 11:28-30; 22:1-14). In the last chapter of the Bible, we find these words: 'And let him who thirsts come. Whoever desires, let him take the water of life freely' (Rev. 22:17). It seems that God refused to close the Bible without offering one more appeal to all.

> 'The only people who will come to him are those who first admit to themselves and to God that they are sinners and need a Saviour'
>
> (Gordon J. Keddie, vol. 1, p.301).

An exclusive appeal: 'let him come to me'

Nothing about Christianity is more objectionable today than its claim that Jesus and Jesus alone is the way of salvation. Let there be no mistake. That exclusivity comes from Jesus himself. He here calls people to himself (see also John 14:6).

An instructive appeal: 'drink'

We receive the Lord Jesus by believing in him even as we receive water by drinking it.

An attractive appeal: 'out of his heart will flow rivers of living water'

When we come in faith to Jesus he both quenches our spiritual thirst and makes us the means of quenching the thirst of others.

> 'Those who were satisfied by him would become themselves sources of spiritual blessing, channels of spiritual life. His truth, his grace, his saving power, would flow through them for the saving and satisfying of other souls. Their influence would not be meager and restricted, but like "rivers of living water"'
>
> (Charles R. Erdman, p.74).

The aftermath of the invitation (vv. 40-52)

Division among the people (vv. 40-44)

Some were captivated by Jesus and spoke a good word for him (vv. 40-41), but that was evidently all they did. Others were prejudiced against Jesus. They knew the Messiah was to come out of Bethlehem in Judah, and they mistakenly assumed that Jesus was from Galilee (vv. 41-42). They can be taken to represent all those who reject Jesus without taking time to investigate his claims. Still others were enraged against Jesus even to the point of wanting to kill him (v. 44).

> 'These men knew where Christ was to be born. They referred to the Scriptures as though familiar with their contents. And yet the eyes of their understanding were not enlightened … Unless our hearts are affected and our lives moulded by God's Word, we are no better off than a starving man with a cook book in his hand'
>
> (Arthur W. Pink, *John*, vol. i, pp.405-6).

The message of Jesus still sounds today and we must also respond. It is not a question of whether we will respond but only how. The above responses are all inadequate. The true response is that of faith.

Division among the religious leaders (vv. 45-52)

1. *The Pharisees and the officers* (vv. 45-49). The officers whom the Pharisees had sent to take Jesus into custody (v. 32) returned empty-handed. When asked to explain their failure, they said, 'No man ever spoke like this Man!' (v. 46). This caused the Pharisees to heap scorn upon them. In addition to accusing them of being deceived, they indicated that they

were out of step with the elite (v. 48) and, as indicated by the word they used for the people (*'oxlos'*), had associated themselves with the dregs of society (v. 49).

2. *Nicodemus and the Pharisees* (vv. 50-52). Here we have evidence that Nicodemus came to true faith on the night that he visited with Jesus (John 3:1-21). His point about the law was correct and bold (v. 51), but it only served to underscore the blindness of his associates who mistakenly assumed Jesus was from Galilee and that no prophet had risen from there (Jonah and Nahum).

> 'They refused to admit that Nicodemus was right in asking for a fair trial, but the only way they could answer him was by means of ridicule. This is an ancient debate trick: when you cannot answer the argument, attack the speaker'
> (Warren W. Wiersbe, *The Bible Exposition Commentary*,
> vol. i, p.318).

We cannot control how people respond to Jesus, but we can hold him forth as the living water of salvation with the confidence that some will receive him.

DIGGING   DEEPER

1. *Read verses 25-31. What is the focus of the debate reported in these verses? How did Jesus respond to it?*

2. *Read verses 32-36. What is the subject of the debate in these verses? Who is involved?*

3. Read verses 37-39. What does Jesus promise here?

4. Read verses 40-44. What conclusions did people draw about Jesus after hearing his invitation?

5. Read verses 45-52. Why had the officers failed to take Jesus into custody? How did the Pharisees respond to their failure?

Find and circle in the puzzle below the four words of a key phrase from this week's lesson.

S	Q	L	R	M	A	Z	D	W	T
W	I	N	I	X	G	I	K	A	U
A	C	J	V	V	Z	Q	D	T	S
P	P	B	E	Z	I	O	F	E	V
C	P	E	R	X	F	N	W	R	X
Y	O	Q	S	T	B	R	G	P	F

A perplexing dilemma and a glorious revelation

'Then Jesus spoke to them again, saying, "I am the light of the world. He who follows me shall not walk in darkness, but have the light of life"' (8:12).

These verses deal with the morning after the conclusion of the Feast of Tabernacles. Having spent the night on the Mount of Olives, Jesus returned early in the morning to the temple in Jerusalem where he began teaching. Suddenly the scribes and Pharisees burst in with a woman whom they claimed had been caught in the act of adultery.

> 'It is common for those that are indulgent to their own sin to be severe against the sins of others'
> (Matthew Henry, vol. v, p.981).

Jesus deals with a dilemma (7:53 - 8:11)

What the law prescribed

1. There were to be multiple witnesses to the act of adultery, not just suspicion of the act.

2. These witnesses were to bring both parties to the Sanhedrin for trial.

3. If the parties were found guilty, the witnesses were to be the first to cast stones at both parties.

What happened on this occasion

1. The scribes and Pharisees brought the woman only.

2. They brought her to Jesus instead of the Sanhedrin. On one hand, Jesus had shown great respect for the law of Moses. He claimed that he had not come to destroy it but to fulfil it. On the other hand, he had shown deep compassion for sinners. In this case the scribes and Pharisees were attempting to force him to embrace one of these two priorities while repudiating the other. The question posed by this case, then, was how could the law be satisfied and the guilty still go free?

> 'Jesus is the one who is really on trial'
>
> (Gordon J. Keddie, vol. 1, p.312).

3. They refused to take the lead in stoning her.

What Jesus did

Various opinions have been offered on why Jesus wrote on the ground and also on what he wrote.

> 'Jesus was simply letting them stew for a bit! Writing in the dirt was no more than a dramatic doodle to heighten the tension. Let them wonder what he would say. Let them speculate about the deeper meaning of his actions — that was just a diversionary tactic, setting them up for a coup de grâce that was about to be administered in plain language!'
>
> (Gordon J. Keddie, vol. 1, p.314).

While we cannot draw a hard and fast conclusion about the writing on the ground, we can say with certainty that Jesus did two things.

1. *He honoured the law.* Gordon J. Keddie writes:

> 'Jesus was not here abrogating any law of God respecting sexual sin. He was in fact upholding that law. He was insisting upon rules of evidence and equal justice'
>
> (vol. 1, p.315).

The problem with the scribes and Pharisees was their selective obedience to the law. They claimed to be champions of it, but they kept only those parts that suited them. In this case, they had again broken the very law they professed to revere.

2. *He let the woman go.* Jesus was not the properly constituted authority for pronouncing sentence upon this woman. If he had done so, he himself would have broken the law. But in letting her go, he did not condone her sin (v. 11).

Unspeakably precious are these words: 'Neither do I condemn you…' ! (v. 11). S. G. DeGraaf writes:

> 'The grace of God burst into the woman's life. She was an outcast; she had deserved to die. However, the Lord Jesus revealed to her that we are all under the guilt of our sins, but through God there is forgiveness'
>
> (*Promise and Deliverance*, vol. iv, p.61).

We have in this episode a stirring picture of the redeeming work of Jesus. The law of God has justly accused each and every one of us of having broken it. Furthermore, it has pronounced the sentence of eternal death upon us. The most urgent of all questions is this: How can both the law of God be satisfied and guilty sinners be set free?

Jesus' death on the cross provides the answer. It honoured the law in that Jesus received the penalty that the law prescribes against sinners. The law only requires that its penalty be paid once. If Jesus paid it, there is no penalty left for those for whom he died. Jesus' death, therefore, both honours the law and sets sinners free.

Jesus reveals himself as the light of the world (8:12)

Here we have the second of the seven 'I am' sayings in this Gospel (see 6:41). What prompted Jesus to speak these words? Some think it was the earliness of the hour (v. 2). They contend that Jesus used the rising of the sun to call attention to the work he came to do. Others believe Jesus' words form a natural conclusion to his conversation with the woman. Having dispelled her darkness, he announces himself as the light for the world.

This saying tells us something about the world that many do not like to hear, namely, it is spiritually and morally dark. Jesus was claiming to dispel this darkness. The fact that Jesus is the light of the world cannot be taken to mean that all are automatically freed from the darkness of sin. Jesus only dispels the darkness for those who follow him.

'To follow Christ is to commit ourselves wholly and entirely to Him as our only leader and Saviour, and to submit ourselves to Him in every matter both of doctrine and practice. "Following" is only another word for "believing". It is the same act of soul, only seen from a different point of view'

(J. C. Ryle, *Thoughts*, vol. 2, p.85).

DIGGING DEEPER

1. *Read the last verse of John 7 and the first verse of John 8. What do these verses teach us about Jesus?*

2. *Read verse 2. What additional information does this verse give us about Jesus?*

3. *Read verses 3-6. Why did the Pharisees bring this woman to Jesus? What conclusions can we draw about them from this act?*

4. *Read verses 7-11. What additional information about Jesus do these verses teach?*

5. *Read verse 12. What do you understand Jesus to be claiming here?*

 From the verses indicated find words to complete the statement of J. C. Ryle about Jesus:

'He has _____ [Matt. 28:6], like the _____ [Mal. 4:2], to diffuse _____ [1 Thess. 5:5], and _____ [Gen. 2:7], and _____ [Rom. 5:1], and _____ [Luke 2:30], in the midst of a _____ [2 Peter 1:19] world'

(J. C. Ryle, vol. 2, p.84).

WEEK 22
John 8:13-29

Jesus converses with the Pharisees

 'And he who sent me is with me. The Father has not left me alone, for I always do those things that please him' (8:29).

With these verses, the apostle John continues his account of Jesus in Jerusalem after the Feast of Tabernacles. The emphasis is on the conversation between Jesus and the Pharisees, which consisted of four parts.

About his testimony (vv. 13-18)

The Pharisees were angered by Jesus claiming to be the light of the world (v. 12). Knowing their own influence would be greatly diminished if the people embraced Jesus, they could not allow such teaching to go unchallenged.

They had already sought to kill him on two occasions (5:16; 7:30). By bringing the woman caught in adultery, they had sought to discredit him (8:1-11). These verses show them trying to overthrow his words on the basis of a technicality.

Jewish law provided that no one could be convicted on the testimony of a single witness, but the Pharisees, as they did with the rest of Moses' law, interpreted and applied this stipulation in a way that distorted the original intent. They had lifted this provision out of the narrow context of the legal system and applied it to all conversation. The result was that nothing could be believed unless more than one person could attest to it.

Jesus responded to this technicality by pointing out two things. Firstly, his claim was something to which no human witness could possibly give testimony (v. 14). He had been sent from heaven and was going back to heaven. Human beings witnessed his birth and his death, but no one had seen him leave heaven and no one would see him re-enter the presence of God.

Secondly, he pointed out that even though no human witness could verify his claim, he still met their requirements. He, Jesus, bore witness to himself. That witness was true because Jesus was in a unique category (v. 14). God the Father also bore witness to him (vv. 16-18), as detailed in John 5:31-47.

About the Father (vv. 19-20)

The Pharisees responded to Jesus' reference to his Father by asking: 'Where is your Father?' (v. 19). This should not be taken as a sincere request for truth. It was their way of dismissing what Jesus had said. It is as if they had said, 'If your Father is your witness, let him show himself now.'

Jesus' reply shows that the problem was not that the witness of the Father was not clear and compelling, it was rather that the Pharisees did not know the Father or the true identity of the Lord Jesus himself (v. 19). Gordon J. Keddie says,

'The facts were plain enough, and still are. The problem is not evidence, but a heart of unbelief that is determined to deny the truth, come what may'

(vol. 1, pp.327-8).

About their destiny (vv. 21-24)

The Pharisees' rejection of Jesus and his Father was no small thing. Three times in these verses, Jesus warns the Pharisees about the terrible possibility of dying in sin.

1. *Dying in sin follows a life of constant searching and never finding* (v. 21). After Jesus' death these men would continue to seek what he and he alone could provide without realizing that he was the provider.

2. *Dying in sin means hopelessness* (vv. 21-23). The word 'cannot' (vv. 21-22) is strong and emphatic. To die without Christ is to give up all hope of entering heaven (Luke 16:26). To die without Christ means going beneath instead of going above to be with him. The Pharisees' mockery of Jesus was hell-inspired, and would take them there if they refused to repent.

3. *Dying in sin means dying unnecessarily* (v. 24). Jesus, the way to eternal life, was right there in front of them. All that was necessary for them to avoid dying in sin was to believe in him.

> 'Believers die in Christ, in his love, in his arms, and so are saved from dying *in their sins*'
> (Matthew Henry, vol. v, p.989, italics are his).

About his identity (vv. 25-29)

The words of Jesus were so strong and forceful that the Pharisees were compelled to ask: 'Who are you?' (v. 25). Jesus had already begun to answer this question before they asked by saying that he was from above (v. 23).

153

After they voiced the question, he tells them that his identity had not changed. He was the same as he had been saying from the beginning (v. 25). And what had he been saying? That he was sent by the Father and spoke the words of the Father, words that would compound their guilt and add to their judgement (v. 26). He would soon add that he was sustained by the Father (vv. 28-29) and obedient to the Father (v. 29). Jesus was the Father's man.

Jesus further answered their question by assuring them that the truth about himself would finally come home to them when he was lifted up on the cross (v. 28).

William Hendriksen explains:

'What Jesus means is that having refused to accept him by faith and having nailed him to the cross ... they would one day awaken to the terrifying realization that this One whom they despised was, nevertheless, whatever he claimed to be. Too late this truth would crash in upon them, in the hour of death and at the final judgment'

(vol. ii, p.48).

DIGGING   DEEPER

1. Read verses 13-18. Why is Jesus' witness of himself true? In what ways had the Father witnessed to Jesus?

2. Read verse 19. What is Jesus' explanation for the Pharisees' rejection of the Father's witness?

3. Read verse 20. Why were Jesus' enemies unable to harm him?

4. *Read verses 21-24. What does it mean to die in sin?*

5. *Read verses 25-29. What do these verses teach about the relationship between the Lord Jesus and the Father?*

Across:

3. Where Jesus was from (v. 23)

4. Those to whom Jesus spoke (v. 13)

6. What the Father is (v. 26)

Down:

1. The one who bears witness of Jesus (v. 18)

2. Where Jesus spoke (v. 20)

5. What the Pharisees would die in (v. 24)

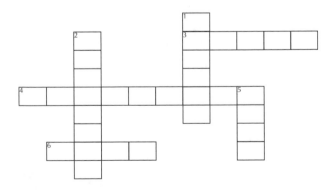

More conflict

'Then Jesus said to those Jews who believed him, "If you abide in my word, you are my disciples indeed"' (8:31).

With these verses the apostle John describes yet another conversation Jesus had while he was in Jerusalem. The conversation begins with 'those Jews who believed him' (v. 31). Since it seems unlikely that the people of verse 30, even if they were false believers, could so quickly and violently turn against Jesus, some think that there is a transition from them to the religious leaders who had made no such profession. This view may be true. As was so often the case, when Jesus spoke to one group, others were present and joined in — see Luke 12:1,13,22,41,54. Others hold that Jesus is addressing the false believers from verse 31 through verse 47.

'...they become furious and no longer *believe* in him in any sense'
(William Hendriksen, vol. ii, p.52, italics are his).

'Probably nothing more is here signified than that they were momentarily impressed so that their enmity against Him was, temporarily, allayed'
(Arthur W. Pink, *John*, vol. ii, p.37).

Jesus responds to a profession (vv. 30-32)

Jesus' exchange with these people makes it clear that we cannot take the word 'believed' at face value. There is a kind of belief that falls far short of the real thing.

Because Jesus had perfect knowledge of all men, he could always detect false belief. And having detected it, he never failed to challenge and test it. He here puts these 'believers' to the test by putting the following sequence before them:

- those who have true faith will continue in Christ's word (v. 31). William Hendriksen explains:

'One abides in the word of Christ by making it the rule of one's life. In other words, *obedience* is the same thing as abiding in the word'

(vol. ii. p.52, italics are his).

- those who continue in Christ's word will know the truth (v. 32). Such continuance means we learn more and more about how God wants us to live, and the more we continue in his word, the more we will be convinced that it is his word and can truly be trusted.

- those who know the truth will experience true freedom (v. 32).

'One is free when sin no longer rules over him, and when the word of Christ dominates his heart and life… One is free, therefore, not when he can do what he wishes to do but when he wishes to do and can do what he should do'

(William Hendriksen, vol. ii, p.52).

'Sin is indeed the hardest of all task masters. Misery and disappointment by the way, despair and hell in the end

— these are the only wages that sin pays to its servants. To deliver men from this bondage is the grand object of the Gospel. To awaken people to a sense of their degradation, to show them their chains, to make them arise and struggle to be free — this is the great end for which Christ sent forth His ministers. Happy is he who has opened his eyes and found out his danger! To know that we are being led captive, is the very first step toward deliverance'

(J. C. Ryle, vol. 2, p.115).

Jesus responds to objections (vv. 33-47)

About true freedom (vv. 33-38)

Jesus' hearers objected to his words. They claimed to be free simply because they were descendants of Abraham. They said they had never been in bondage to anyone, yet they were at that very moment in bondage to Rome. Little did they realize it, but they were also in bondage to sin.

Jesus responded by pointing out that the kind of freedom he had offered was freedom from sin (vv. 34-36). Their lives gave abundant evidence that they were the slaves of sin, and as slaves they were in a precarious position. Slaves have no security. Their great need, therefore, was to become sons of God. Only then would they have security and freedom. How does a slave become a son? The Son of God is the only one who can make us sons (or daughters) of God (v. 36).

About having Abraham as their father (vv. 39-41)

We are familiar with the phrase 'like father, like son'. Children do take after their parents. Using that principle,

Jesus essentially told his hearers that they had to learn to act like Abraham before they could legitimately claim him as their father.

'The profession of our lips amounts to nothing at all if it be not confirmed by the character of our lives. Talk is cheap; it is our works, what we *do*, which evidences what we really *are*. A tree is known by its fruits'
(Arthur W. Pink, vol. ii, p.47, italics are his).

The issue here is, of course, spiritual descent. Yes, they had physically descended from Abraham, but they certainly were not his spiritual descendants. While Abraham demonstrated a hospitality for the messengers of God and the truth they came to deliver (Gen. 18:1-8), the Word of Christ had 'no place' in the lives of Jesus' listeners. Jesus forcefully asserted that they most certainly did the deeds of their father, but he did not specify at this point who was their father (v. 41).

About having God as their Father (vv. 41-47)

The fact that Jesus did not say whom he had in mind when he talked about their father (v. 41) further angered these people. Had he suggested that they were born of fornication (v. 41), that is, that their father could not be identified? They were finally ready to move from the matter of physical descent to spiritual descent. It is as if they said, 'You may have doubts about our physical lineage, but you cannot question our spiritual lineage. We have God as our Father.'

Jesus responded to that statement with the same inexorable logic he used when they claimed Abraham as their father. Their deeds indicated otherwise! If evil deeds were out of keeping with Abraham, they were even more so with God.

At this point and on the basis of their deeds, Jesus identified their father — Satan himself (v. 44). Did they have hatred and murder in their hearts? Yes! They wanted to kill Jesus (vv. 37,40). Were they lying? Yes! They were lying to themselves about what was in their hearts. The one from whom such things spring is Satan. Therefore, he had to be their father.

This passage is not merely an account of a very old religious conflict. It puts before us matters of tremendous significance. It speaks in particular about the importance of having the proper attitude towards the Word of God (note the phrases pertaining to the word in verses 31,37,43,47).

DIGGING DEEPER

1. *Read verses 30-32. What will characterize those who truly believe in Jesus?*

2. *Read verses 33-36. Of what does true freedom consist?*

3. *Read verses 37-43. How does one show to whom he spiritually belongs?*

4. *Read verse 44. What two words describe Satan?*

5. *Read verses 45-47. What characterizes those in whom God does his saving work?*

Each of the verses below uses the word 'abide' or 'continue'. Beside each verse write that in which God's people are to continue.

John 15:9 _____

Romans 11:22 _____

Colossians 1:23 _____

Colossians 4:2 _____

Hebrews 13:1 _____

Complete the following verse: 'They went out from us, but they were not of us; for if they had been of us, they would have _____ with us; but they went out that they might be made manifest, that none of them were of us' (1 John 2:19).

WEEK 24

John 8:48-59

Hostility for Jesus

'Jesus said to them, "Most assuredly, I say to you, before Abraham was, I AM"' (8:58).

The conversation recorded in these verses shows us the deep hostility the religious leaders had for Jesus. This passage shows them manifesting their opposition by making false accusations, and increasing their hostility even more because of what Jesus said regarding Abraham.

Jesus and false accusations (vv. 48-52)

The accusations

1. *Jesus was a Samaritan* (v. 48). The Samaritans were a racially mixed people who were despised and hated by pure-blooded Jews. They were suggesting, therefore, that Jesus was not truly Jewish and had no authority to speak to them. He was rather a traitor to the Jewish nation who would delight in doing it great harm.

   In saying this, the religious leaders were only revealing how they felt about Samaritans. Jesus did not hate the

Samaritans but saw them as he saw everyone else, as sinners in need of the gift of eternal life (John 4).

2. *Jesus was demon-possessed* (v. 48). In their estimation the only thing worse than being a Samaritan was being a demon-possessed Samaritan. The intensity of their hatred is shown by the fact that they repeat this charge in verse 52. In verse 53, they suggest that his demon-possession had led him into delusions of grandeur.

3. *Jesus was commonly regarded in the above ways* (v. 48). The phrase 'do we not say rightly' implies that whenever people talked about Jesus, they were always saying the same things the leaders themselves had just said. It is bad enough for someone to say, 'I think you are crazy.' It is worse when he says, 'Everyone in town thinks you are crazy!' This is what the religious leaders were saying to Jesus.

These accusations should cause us to marvel at what Jesus did in order to win our redemption. How far he had to stoop! He left the glories of heaven where he was the object of adoration and praise, and came all the way to earth to be disdained by sinners. What burdens he had to bear to save us!

Jesus' answer

1. He gave an *explanation* of his ministry (vv. 49-50). Jesus conducted his life in terms of what would please God. When he healed the lame man, he was doing the work of God (5:17). When he claimed to be the light of the world, he spoke as the Father wanted (8:14,18).

2. He pointed to the final *vindication* of his ministry (v. 50). What the religious leaders thought and said did not matter. God has already determined that every knee is going to

finally bend before Jesus and every tongue is going to finally confess that he is Lord over all (Phil. 2:9-11).

3. Jesus issued a gracious *invitation* (v. 51). Jesus would have been justified in destroying these men on the spot. Instead he told them that they could be spared from seeing eternal death (vv. 21,24) if they would heed his message.

> '...*if a man* ... receives the Gospel in the love of it, obeys it from his heart, and cordially embraces and firmly believes it; and retains and holds it fast, having a spiritual and comfortable experience of the doctrines of Christ, and yielding a cheerful and ready obedience to his commands and ordinances, in faith and love: *he shall never see death*; the second death, eternal death, which is an everlasting separation of a man, body and soul, from God; this death shall have no power on such a person, he shall never be hurt by it...'
>
> (John Gill, *Exposition of the Old and New Testaments*,
> vol. viii, p.853, italics are his).

In the answer Jesus gave to these religious leaders we have the keys to how we are to handle opposition ourselves.

1. Like Jesus, we must have a firm hold on the honour of God as the non-negotiable, guiding principle in our lives. In other words, we cannot let opposition from the world cause us to lower our standards. The Christian is one who has been called out of this world for the express purpose of showing forth the praises of God (1 Peter 2:9-10), and no amount of opposition from the world can change the Christian's obligation to live for this purpose.

2. As Jesus looked past the insults of the religious leaders to his ultimate vindication from God, so must we look to that

time when the trials of life will be over and Christians will be proved to be right in their faith and will shine forth as the stars of the firmament.

3. As Jesus met the insults of the religious leaders with a gracious invitation to believe, so we must continue to hold forth the Word of life to the very people who oppose us.

Jesus and Abraham (vv. 53-59)

The religious leaders misunderstood Jesus' promise that those who keep his word will 'never see death' (v. 51). They assumed he was referring to physical death. The greatest people in their history, Abraham and the prophets, had all died. These great people could not escape death themselves, and now Jesus was claiming to be the means of escape for others. He was obviously claiming to be greater than Abraham (v. 53). This was intolerable!

Jesus responded by asserting the following:

- They, the religious leaders, were wrong to think that he was making these claims out of a desire to promote and glorify himself. Jesus lived in complete submission to the Father and could, therefore, leave his honour with the Father (vv. 54-55).

  'If we really know the Father it will be evidenced by our subjection to His Word!'
  (Arthur W. Pink, vol. ii, p.55).

- He was greater than Abraham (vv. 56-59). Jesus was the fulfilment of the promises made to Abraham, who saw the coming of Jesus and 'was glad' (v. 56).

166

'The plain truth is, that we are too apt to forget that there never was but one way of salvation, one Saviour, and one hope for sinners, and that Abraham and all the Old Testament saints looked to the same Christ that we look to ourselves'
(J. C. Ryle, vol. 2, p.139).

But Jesus did not merely come after Abraham. He was before him (v. 58). When Jesus appropriated the words 'I AM' to himself, it was more than his listeners could bear. God himself had spoken those words to Moses at the burning bush (Exod. 3:14). In using those same words, the Lord revealed that he has always been, is and always will be. Jesus was claiming to be the eternal God in human flesh! At this point, these religious leaders decided to end the debate by putting an end to Jesus.

'To a generation conscious of the brevity of life, and in a culture where time is replacing money as the commodity of highest value, we feel constantly threatened by time's flow. It runs through our fingers and escapes no matter how frantically we try to fill it and hold it back. But Christ has all time in his hands; and as we rest our lives in him our fragile, ephemeral consciousness finds meaning and permanence'
(Bruce Milne, *The Message of John*, p.136).

DIGGING DEEPER

1. *Read verse 48. What insults did the religious leaders hurl at Jesus?*

2. *Read verses 49-51. How did Jesus respond to these insults?*

3. *Read verses 52-53. Why did the religious leaders conclude that Jesus was claiming to be greater than Abraham?*

4. *Read verses 54-58. On what grounds did Jesus claim to be greater than Abraham?*

5. *Read verse 59. How did the religious leaders respond to Jesus' claims?*

Use the first letters of the missing words in the verses below to find a key word in this week's lesson:

'...through whom also we have _____ by faith into this grace in which we stand, and rejoice in hope of the glory of God' (Rom. 5:2).

'...that at the name of Jesus every knee should _____, of those in heaven and of those on earth, and of those under the earth...' (Phil. 2:10).

'The LORD _____, he is clothed with majesty...' (Ps. 93:1).

'The effective, fervent prayer of a righteous man _____ much' (James 5:16).

'Therefore, holy brethren, partakers of the _____ calling, consider the Apostle and High Priest of our confession, Christ Jesus' (Heb. 3:1).

'I shall be satisfied when I _____ in your likeness' (Ps. 17:15).

'Therefore be _____, just as your Father also is merciful' (Luke 6:36).

KEY WORD: ___ ___ ___ ___ ___ ___ ___

The man born blind

'I must work the works of him who sent me while it is day; the night is coming when no one can work' (9:4).

John 8 concludes with Jesus passing by the religious leaders (8:59). It opens with Jesus passing by the blind man. His passing by the leaders was an act of judgement; his passing by the blind man was an act of grace. Jesus passes all of us in either grace or in judgement.

The healing of this man constitutes the sixth of the seven signs recorded by John.

Jesus answers his disciples (vv. 1-5)

When they saw this blind man, Jesus' disciples could only think of two explanations: either the man was being punished for sinning or his parents had committed a grievous sin. While all suffering must ultimately be attributed to sin, we must not say that each case of suffering is caused by a specific sin. Sometimes this is true, but it is not true in every case.

Jesus said this man's suffering was not due to a specific sin. It was rather designed by God for a specific purpose:

'that the works of God should be revealed in him' (v. 3). This man's blindness had been designed for the very moment described in these verses — that moment when Jesus would heal him! Does this constitute something of a raw deal? Not at all. Firstly, this man's story has brought inspiration and comfort to countless numbers. Secondly, his physical healing led to his spiritual healing.

Another example of this teaching is found in John 11. There Jesus allowed Lazarus to die so that he, Jesus, could demonstrate his glory by raising him (11:4).

It is interesting that Jesus quickly moved from the theological dilemma posed by this man to the work that he, Jesus, had come to do. He points out the urgency of this work ('while it is day', v. 4).

The most important point we need to grasp is that there will be an eternity for us to have our questions answered, but this life offers us a very limited time to work for the Lord. Some may wonder if this verse applies to us in that Jesus was speaking about himself and his work. But the servant is not greater than his master. If the Lord Jesus had work to do, we may rest assured that we do as well.

The things Jesus says here about his approach to his work ought to give pause for thought to all who are his followers. Do we apply ourselves to the tasks he has assigned us with faithfulness? Do we see that our time here is fleeting and that we must work with a sense of urgency?

'The life that we now live in the flesh is our day. Let us take care that we use it well, for the glory of God and the good of our souls. Let us work out our salvation with fear and trembling, while it is called today. There is no work nor labour in the grave, toward which we are all fast hastening. Let us pray, and read, and keep our Sabbaths holy, and hear God's Word, and do good in our generation, like men who

never forget that "the night is at hand". Our time is very short.
Our daylight will soon be gone. Opportunities once lost can
never be retrieved'

(J. C. Ryle, vol. 2, pp.152-3).

Jesus heals the blind man (vv. 6-7)

After responding to the disciples' question, Jesus proceeded
to make a mudpack, put it on the eyes of the blind man and
then told him to go and wash in the pool of Siloam.

What was the purpose of the spit and clay? To outward
appearances, this combination was offensive and inadequate.
But in the hands of Jesus it was effective. In like manner, the
cross of Christ appears to be offensive and inadequate in
bringing eternal salvation. But in the plan and purpose of
God, that cross is effective (1 Cor. 1:18-25).

What was the purpose of the pool? The word 'Siloam'
means 'sent'. It is the same word as 'Shiloh' in Genesis 49:10,
which is a prophecy of Christ.

William Hendriksen says,

'... [the] deeper meaning is surely this: that for spiritual
cleansing one must go to the true Siloam; i.e., to the One
who was sent by the Father to save sinners'

(vol. ii, p.76).

'Christ is often called the *sent of God* ... so that when Christ
sent him to the pool of Siloam he did in effect send him to
himself; for Christ is *all in all* to the healing of souls. Christ as
a prophet directs us to himself as a priest'

(Matthew Henry, vol. v, pp.1012-3).

The man explains his healing (vv. 8-17)

To his acquaintances (vv. 8-12)

The neighbours of the man, who knew him best, confirmed that this was indeed the man they knew, but they wondered how he could now see. Those who had 'previously seen him' (v. 8) probably refers to people who had simply passed him on several occasions. They were uncertain about whether the man they were now seeing was the one they had seen before.

The curiosity of these people gave the man the opportunity to tell them what had taken place. This he did in simple, straightforward fashion (v. 11). Every Christian should respond to opportunities to witness for Christ in the same way.

To the Pharisees (vv. 13-17)

The Pharisees were outraged by this healing because Jesus had carried it out on the Sabbath. Not only had he performed work by making the mudpack, but the work was also unnecessary (the man could have stayed blind one more day!). While others were divided about Jesus, the healed man was certain that Jesus had made him see (v. 15) and was, therefore, a prophet (v. 17).

> 'The Pharisees were ... in a dilemma; there stood the man; his sight was perfect; he had been born blind; Jesus had opened his eyes. They must either deny the facts or admit the divine nature of Jesus which the facts proved'
> (Charles R. Erdman, pp.87-8).

DIGGING DEEPER

1. *Read verses 1-3. How did the disciples explain this man's blindness? How did Jesus explain it?*

2. *Read verses 4-5. How did Jesus explain his presence in this world?*

3. *Read verses 6-7. What did Jesus require of the blind man?*

4. *Read verses 8-12. What issues are debated here?*

5. *Read verses 13-17. What conclusion did the Pharisees draw about Jesus?*

Jesus' use of spit and clay reminds us that God often uses unlikely instruments to accomplish his purposes. From the Scriptures listed below identify in the appropriate blanks the problem and the means God used to resolve it.

Problem   Means

_____ (Num. 21:4-9) _____

_____ (Josh. 6:1-5) _____

Problem   Means

_____ (1 Sam. 17:4-7,49-50) _____

_____ (2 Kings 2:19-22) _____

_____ (1 Cor. 1:18-21) _____

Controversy over a healing

'Then he said, "Lord, I believe!" And he worshipped him' (9:38).

We might be inclined to think that the healing of a man blind from birth would be the cause of great rejoicing, but it only caused more controversy. We can divide John's account of this controversy into three parts.

The healed man defends Jesus (vv. 18-34)

The arguments of the Pharisees (vv. 24,26,28-29)

The religious leaders used three arguments to get around the evidence for the healing:

1. *'Nothing happened'* (v. 18). Desperate to find a way to get around the miracle, the Pharisees met with the man's parents. They were evidently hoping to prove that he had not really been blind at all. Or perhaps they were hoping that the man who claimed to be healed was actually a seeing man who looked like their son. They may have been hoping that Jesus saw the resemblance, and convinced this man to be 'healed'.

2. *'Something happened but not what this man thinks'* (v. 24).
They suggested the man had been healed, but not through
the power of Jesus. God had done it for him, and Jesus,
they argued, just happened to be there fiddling with the
mud.

3. *'No one can know for sure what happened'* (v. 29).

The real problem was that these leaders had drawn
their conclusion before looking at the evidence. With that
conclusion firmly planted, they would not let the evidence
speak for itself but rather looked for a way to get around
it. Their strategies are still used against those who claim to
have been changed by Christ.

The answers of the healed man (vv. 25,27)

The healed man, refusing to be swayed by the religious
leaders, made three truths clear:

1. A dramatic change had taken place (v. 25);

2. It had taken place at the command of Jesus (vv. 25,30);

3. It was of such a nature that it could only be explained as
   an act of God (v. 33).

Jesus heals the healed man (vv. 35-38)

These verses relate Jesus' second encounter with this man.
While the first encounter produced physical healing, this
one produced spiritual healing. The man became a believer
in Jesus.

We should note that this spiritual healing took place as a result of Jesus seeking this man (v. 35) and revealing the truth to him (v. 37). The man responded to the truth by crying: 'Lord, I believe!' Some equate believing with intellectual assent. They think they are right with God because they accept as facts the existence of God and Jesus. But the word 'believe' always carries the idea of commitment with it. Therefore, when we read that this man believed, we are to understand that he entrusted himself completely to Jesus as his Saviour and Lord.

It is obvious that Jesus intended the physical healing of this man to culminate in his spiritual healing. The one was a picture of the other. These healings yield the following conclusions about salvation:

- As this man was physically blind and totally unable to help himself, we are all by nature spiritually blind and helpless (2 Cor. 4:4).

- As this man was physically healed by the grace and power of Jesus, we are spiritually healed by the same means (Eph. 2:8-9).

- As Jesus used seemingly inadequate and absurd means (clay, spit, the pool) to heal this man, he uses his seemingly inadequate and absurd death on the cross to provide salvation (1 Cor. 1:18-25).

- As this man was spiritually healed by believing on Jesus we are saved in the same way. What does it mean to believe in Jesus? True belief consists of knowing the facts about Jesus, believing those facts are true and trusting in or relying upon those facts for salvation. True belief always involves commitment.

- As this man readily obeyed Jesus' commands (v. 7) and eagerly worshipped him (v. 38), so those who are saved will desire to obey the Lord and to worship Christ.

- As this man encountered opposition because of the change he experienced, so believers in Christ can expect opposition because of the spiritual change he has made in their lives (2 Tim. 3:12).

Jesus confronts the Pharisees (vv. 39-41)

When the Pharisees heard Jesus say that he had come so that those who see would be made blind, they knew he was referring to them. They were the ones who claimed to see. They claimed to have spiritual knowledge and to be the spiritual leaders of Israel.

Always eager to do battle with Jesus, they sarcastically responded: 'Are we blind also?' (v. 40). They were essentially asking Jesus: 'Are you insinuating that we are blind, that we do not have spiritual knowledge?'

They expected Jesus to say: 'Yes, you are blind.' He surprised them by saying: 'If only you were blind, all would be well.'

As Jesus had powerfully demonstrated, blind men can be made to see. But what can be done for the one who refuses to admit that he is blind? This was the very core of the Pharisees' problem. As far as they were concerned, they had no spiritual need and, therefore, did not need any help. They thought they had no sin. So they needed no Saviour. If they had only been willing to be blind, they could have been made to see. If they been willing to be sinners, they could have been saved. As it was, they refused to admit their sin, so their sin remained.

Arthur W. Pink paraphrases the message of Jesus to the Pharisees:

'If you were sensible of your blindness and really desire light, if you would take this place before Me, salvation would be yours and no condemnation would rest upon you. But because of your pride and self-sufficiency, because you refuse to acknowledge your undone condition, your guilt remaineth'

(vol. ii, p.99).

DIGGING   DEEPER

1. *Read verses 18-23. Why did the Pharisees meet with the parents of the man? How did his parents respond?*

2. *Read verses 24-34. What conclusions did the Pharisees offer about Jesus? How did the blind man respond to each?*

3. *Read verses 35-38. What takes place here?*

4. *Read verses 39-41. What did Jesus say here about his mission? What did he say about the Pharisees?*

Read the following verses and indicate in the blank provided the words that occur in each:

Mark 9:24; John 11:27; Acts 8:37; 27:25.

_____.

Third Quarter

Jesus' teaching on true shepherds

'I am the door. If anyone enters by me, he will be saved, and will go in and out and find pasture' (10:9).

This lesson brings us to two more of Jesus' 'I am' sayings. In verses 7 and 9, he says, 'I am the door.' In verses 11 and 14, he says, 'I am the good shepherd.'

We must keep in mind the background or the context of these two sayings. They come hard on the heels of the Pharisees expelling from the synagogue the man whom Jesus healed of blindness. What had this man done to warrant such action? He had simply registered his conviction that Jesus was sent from God (9:33-34).

The Pharisees professed to be the spiritual shepherds of the people of Israel, but this act proved they weren't true shepherds at all. In the verses of this lesson, Jesus gives two tests of the true shepherd.

The true shepherd recognizes Jesus as the door to the sheepfold (vv. 1-10)

With the imagery of the door, Jesus asserted that he is the measuring rod or the standard in determining whether a man is a true minister or not. The true minister is one who uses the door, Jesus. Entering by the door into the sheepfold, the true minister is recognized by the sheep and is able to lead them. In other words, the true minister is Christ-centred. He has received Jesus as Lord and Saviour and now preaches Christ to others. For their part, the people of God instinctively know the Christ-centred man is of God and they follow him.

The false minister, on the other hand, does not use the door. He does not preach the coming and dying of Christ as the only means of salvation, and he does not seek to glorify and exalt Christ. He tries to get the sheep to follow him by approaching them through some way other than Christ. The final result of this approach is death. That's the reason Jesus says the thief kills and destroys (v. 10). Any ministry that does not preach Christ does not save souls but kills them.

Some have thought that Jesus mixed his metaphors in verses 1-9, that he claims to be both the door and the shepherd in those verses. But the two metaphors are distinct and separate. In verses 1-9, Jesus is the door and the shepherds are ministers. This is indicated by the fact that there is no definite article before the word 'shepherd' in verse 2. When the Bible refers to the Lord Jesus as a shepherd it is always in a definite and special way. In the passage before us, Jesus adds the qualifying word 'good' when he speaks of himself as a shepherd. We find the same thing in other New Testament passages (Heb. 13:20; 1 Peter 5:4).

The great truth these first nine verses teach is that all who profess to be true, spiritual shepherds are not necessarily so. The true shepherd has certain characteristics, the major one being that he makes use of the door, Christ! He has entered the door himself, and he leads others to do the same (v. 2).

'Ordination is no proof whatever that a man is fit to show others the way to heaven. He may have been regularly set apart by those who have authority to call ministers, and yet all his life may never come near the door... The true shepherd of souls is he who enters the ministry with a single eye to Christ, desiring to glorify Christ, doing all in the strength of Christ, preaching Christ's doctrine, walking in Christ's steps, and labouring to bring men and women to Christ. The false shepherd of souls is he who enters the ministerial office with little or no thought about Christ, from worldly and self-exalting motives, but from no desire to exalt Jesus, and the great salvation that is in Him. Christ, in one word, is the grand touchstone of the minister of religion'

(J. C. Ryle, vol. 2, pp.196-7).

The true shepherd exhibits other characteristics as well. He has a deep concern for the spiritual well-being of each one of his sheep (he calls them 'by name', v. 3). Furthermore, he leads by example (he 'leads them out', v. 3). Finally, the true shepherd feeds his flock ('out' in verse 3 implies that he takes them out of the sheepfold to the pastures).

False shepherds do not exhibit these characteristics. The saddest part of false ministry is that it has no door in it (no way of salvation). In addition to this, the false shepherds have no interest in the sheep but simply use them for their own gain. They are, therefore, thieves and robbers.

The true shepherd recognizes Jesus as the good shepherd (vv. 11-21)

Here the Lord drops the figure of the door and speaks of himself as the good shepherd, thus showing the difference between the Pharisees and himself. Men may indeed shepherd the people of God, but they are at their best only undershepherds. The true shepherd under whom they serve is Christ. He is the one to whom the sheep belong.

'Note, Jesus Christ is the best of shepherds, the best in the world to take the over-sight of souls, none so skilful, so faithful, so tender, as he, no such feeder and leader, no such protector and healer of souls as he'

(Matthew Henry, vol. v, p.1031).

What Jesus was concerned about

Firstly, notice what Jesus, as the good shepherd, is concerned about — the life of his sheep (v. 10). The Pharisees did not have the spiritual well-being of others at heart but were thieves and robbers. In pursuing their own selfish ambitions, they actually destroyed the spiritual well-being of others. Here is another good way to determine whether a minister is truly of God. Does he have the spiritual welfare of others at heart or does he ignore spiritual life in his pursuit of lesser priorities? The sad truth is that many ministers have become almost exclusively concerned with how to live in this world and have very little to say about the salvation of the soul at all. And when they do have something to say about it, it is something other than what the Bible says.

What his concern compelled him to do

Four times Jesus says he was going to 'give' or 'lay down' his life for his sheep (vv. 11,15,17,18). Now it was not often the case where his concern for the sheep caused the shepherd to lose his own life. But it was different with Jesus. The life of his flock demanded his own life. In this matter of spiritual life, we were absolutely helpless (Rom. 5:6). There was no way for Jesus to secure the life of his flock apart from giving up his own.

The true undershepherd understands that Jesus was so concerned about his sheep having spiritual life (v. 10) that he gave up his own life for them (v. 11).

> '...in ordinary life the death of the herder means loss and possible death for the herd. In this case the death of the shepherd means life for the sheep!'
>
> (William Hendriksen, vol. ii, p.110).

The nature of his death

This brings us to the nature of our Lord's death.

1. *It was substitutionary.* His death was instead of the death of the sheep. A blow was about to fall upon them, but he interposed himself and took the blow.

2. *It was voluntary* (vv. 15,17-18). When Jesus died on the cross his enemies certainly thought they were taking his life from him; but nothing could have been farther from the truth. There on the cross the Lord was voluntarily laying down his life to purchase our redemption. When the Roman procurator, Pilate, accorded himself too large a role in the crucifixion, the Lord Jesus quickly set the record straight: 'You could have no power at all against me unless it had been given you from above' (John 19:11).

3. *It was victorious.* When Jesus laid his life down it was not in defeat but rather so he could take it up again in the resurrection (vv. 17-18). When Joseph of Arimathea took the body of Jesus and placed it in his own tomb, the enemies of Jesus thought they were finally through with him. They

thought the crucifixion was the last word about Jesus. But the Lord Jesus went to the cross knowing that he would rise from the dead. He says he was laying down his life that he might 'take it again' (vv. 17-18). If Jesus had just died, his death would have had no value for the sheep. The fact that he arose again means he ascended to the Father and sent the Holy Spirit to apply the benefits of his death to his flock.

4. *It was co-operative.* Jesus mentions the Father four times in verses 15-18. His death was not something he did on his own. It was part of the plan that was worked out with his Father before the world began. And the Father took special delight in seeing his Son work out in minute detail on the stage of history what they had so carefully planned in eternity.

5. *It was effective* (v. 16). His death would reach far beyond the narrow confines of the Jewish nation and bring Gentiles into his kingdom (v. 16).

> 'Jesus would give His life not only for His people in Israel but also for people from among all the nations of the world. From among those nations the Father had given Him were many who at that moment had never heard of Him. According to the Father's decree they were already His sheep even though they were from another flock than the people of Israel'
>
> (S. G. DeGraaf, vol. iv, p.70).

To see how powerful and effective the death of Jesus is all we have to do is look at the final book of the Bible. There we find a vast throng gathered around the throne singing these words: 'You were slain, and have redeemed us to God by your blood out of every tribe and tongue and people and nation' (Rev. 5:9).

All of this created another glaring contrast between Jesus and the Pharisees. Jesus came to die for the sheep, but the Pharisees were like hired hands. When danger confronted the sheep, the last thing the hired hand was going to do was put his life on the line. He cared nothing about the sheep. What if the wolf *did* slaughter them? It was no skin off his nose.

We live in a world in which competing voices constantly tell us what is good for us. There is no shortage of those who would shepherd us. But many, like the Pharisees of Jesus' day, have no real concern for the spiritual well-being of our souls. They are interested only in furthering their own agendas. Thank God, there is one who came to give what we so urgently need — abundant life.

What should our response be to all of this? It depends on where we are spiritually. If we would have this abundant life, we must repent of our sins and cast ourselves completely upon Jesus as our only hope for salvation. If we already have this abundant life, we should be thankful and rejoice.

The words of Jesus created division among his hearers. Some accused him of being demon-possessed (vv. 19-20), while others recognized that such gracious words and such a powerful healing (9:1-7) could not possibly come from one who was demon-possessed.

> 'Since Jesus Christ is "the Door", we would expect a division, because a door shuts some people in and others out! He is the Good Shepherd, and the shepherd must separate the sheep from the goats. It is impossible to be neutral about Jesus Christ; for, what we believe about Him is a matter of life and death...'
>
> (Warren W. Wiersbe, *The Bible Exposition Commentary*, vol. i, p.331).

DIGGING   DEEPER

1. *Read verses 1-2. What do these verses tell us about false shepherds and true shepherds?*

2. *Read verses 3-5. How do the sheep respond to the true shepherd?*

3. *Read verse 6. How did Jesus' hearers respond to his remarks?*

4. *Read verses 7-9? How does Jesus identify himself here? What does he promise in these verses?*

5. *Read verses 10-13. How does Jesus identify himself here? How is he different in this capacity from others?*

6. *Read verses 14-18. What does Jesus say here about laying down his life?*

7. *Read verses 19-21. How did the people respond to Jesus?*

Psalm 23 pictures the shepherdly work of the Lord Jesus Christ. In the blanks provided, write a summary of what the Lord Jesus does for his sheep.

_____

_____

_____

_____

In and out of Jerusalem

'My sheep hear my voice, and I know them, and they follow me' (10:27).

After speaking the words recorded in verses 1-18, Jesus apparently departed from Jerusalem. Two months later, he returned for the Feast of Dedication (v. 22). This feast, also known as the Feast of Lights (Hanukkah), was celebrated each December for a period of eight days. It commemorated the purification and rededication of the temple by Judas Maccabaeus in 164 B.C. after it had been defiled by Antiochus Epiphanes, the Seleucid ruler who took control of Israel in 198 B.C.

The fact that this feast was in December — the cold, rainy season — may explain why Jesus was walking in the covered portion of the temple.

Jesus responds to a demand (vv. 22-30)

As Jesus was walking, he suddenly found himself surrounded by the religious leaders of Jerusalem who said, 'How long do you keep us in doubt? If you are the Christ, tell us plainly' (v. 24).

We should not conclude that these men were sincerely seeking the truth and were prepared to accept it. Nothing could be farther from reality. They had long since made up their minds about Jesus, and they were filled with hatred for him. They only asked this question to set a trap for him. If he openly affirmed his messiahship, they would again accuse him of blasphemy. Jesus answered them by pointing out:

- The miracles that he had performed (5:1-9; 9:1-7) spoke plainly enough about his identity (v. 25).

- Their refusal to believe was not due to lack of evidence but rather to the fact that they were not of his sheep (v. 26). The term 'sheep' refers to those who belong to Jesus, those who are utterly helpless left to themselves and totally dependent upon him.

1. *The sheep hear his voice* (v. 27). They heard his voice calling them to salvation, and they continue to listen to his voice as he calls them to obedience.

'They delight in it, are in their element when they are sitting at his feet to hear his word. They do according to it, and make his word their rule. Christ will not account those his sheep that are deaf to his calls, deaf to his charms...'
(Matthew Henry, vol. v, p.1036).

2. *The Lord knows them* (v. 27). He intimately knows each believer and has from eternity past!

3. *They follow him* (v. 27). They not only hear his voice calling them but also obey it. They do not perfectly obey. Sheep stray. But they generally follow, and straying is the exception. So it is with those who truly know Christ.

'...they submit to his guidance by a willing obedience to all his commands, and a cheerful conformity to his spirit and pattern'

(Matthew Henry, vol. v, p.1036).

4. *They receive eternal life from Jesus* (vv. 28-30). The Lord Jesus came to this earth for the purpose of shepherding the flock given to him by God all the way from this earth to heaven itself!

The Lord's shepherding work is so complete and sure that it cannot be thwarted or defeated. His people will 'never perish' (v. 28). They are the recipients of a double-keeping, being in the hand of Christ the Son and simultaneously in the hand of God the Father (vv. 28-29). Those hands are so strong that no one can pluck a single saint from them (v. 29). This double-keeping stems from the oneness and complete equality of the Father and the Son (v. 30).

Jesus responds to a threat (vv. 31-39)

The religious leaders correctly understood that Jesus was claiming to be God (v. 33), and took up stones to kill him.

'Daring sinners will throw stones at heaven, though they return upon their own heads; and will strengthen themselves against the Almighty, though none ever hardened themselves against him and prospered'

(Matthew Henry, vol. v, p.1038).

The law of Moses required that blasphemers be stoned (Lev. 24:16). But Jesus had not blasphemed, he had only spoken the truth. He was God in human flesh! He calmly responded to their rage by:

- affirming something that was undeniably true — the works he had done were good works (v. 32);

- asking an embarrassing question — for which of these good works did they want to stone him? (v. 32);

- by referring them to Scripture (vv. 34-38).

Charles R. Erdman explains Jesus' reference in this way:

'...if the judges, who represented Jehovah in their appointed office, could be called "gods", in the Hebrew scriptures, it could not be blasphemy for him, who was the final and complete revelation of God, to call himself "the Son of God"'

(pp.95-6).

In offering this argument, Jesus was also giving testimony to the divine nature of Scripture. The term 'broken' was one with which his hearers were familiar. When rabbis came together, one would offer his interpretation of some point and the others would then say the argument could be broken, that is, had a weakness or flaw in it. If they could not find any weakness, they would say that it could not be broken. In using this term, Jesus was emphatically affirming that Scripture has no weaknesses or flaws. It cannot be shown at any point to be wrong.

'The term "broken" ... means ... Scripture cannot be emptied of its force by being shown to be erroneous'
(Leon Morris, The Gospel According to John, p.527).

Jesus receives new believers (vv. 40-42)

The ministry that Jesus conducted 'beyond the Jordan' leads to these valuable conclusions:

* No place is too small for God to work.

* No faithful ministry will go unrewarded.

The ministry of John the Baptist continued to have beneficial results. Many came to Jesus because they saw John's message confirmed and verified in Jesus' words and actions.

> 'The last word of our text is the word "there". "Many", we are told, "believed on him there." And where was that? Obviously, where they were and without delay! ... Spurgeon once wrote on this last word of the text: "The devil wants you to wait, for he knows that he can then come and steal away the good seed of the kingdom; but if the Lord should give you the grace to decide for Him at once, if you were to believe on Jesus now, what joy there would be among the angels, and the spirit of just men made perfect! ... What peace there would be in your own heart; and what thankfulness and delight there would be among the people of God when they heard of it"'
>
> (James Montgomery Boice, *John*, p.693).

DIGGING DEEPER

1. Read verses 22-23. What details about Jesus do these verses provide?

197

2. *Read verses 24-26. What reason did Jesus give for the refusal of the religious leaders to believe in him?*

3. *Read verses 27-30. What characteristics of Jesus' sheep does our Lord mention here?*

4. *Read verses 31-33. What reason did the religious leaders give for wanting to stone Jesus?*

5. *Read verses 34-36. What does Jesus assume about the nature of Scripture in these verses?*

6. *Read verses 37-39. What evidence does Jesus give for his claims? How do the religious leaders respond?*

7. *Read verses 40-42. What details about the ministry of Jesus do these verses provide?*

Read Matthew 4:1-11; 5:17-18; Mark 12:18-27 for more information about how Jesus regarded Scripture. In the blanks provided write 'J' beside each word that reflects Jesus' view of Scripture.

_____ Authoritative
_____ Mistaken
_____ Incorrect
_____ Reliable
_____ Trustworthy
_____ Flawed
_____ Contradictory
_____ True

Jesus delays going to Bethany

'When Jesus heard that, he said, "This sickness is not unto death, but for the glory of God, that the Son of God may be glorified through it"' (v. 4).

This long chapter reports the death and resurrection of Lazarus. It also reports the determination of the religious leaders to remove Jesus. Through it all we see the grace and power of the Lord Jesus.

Jesus receives a message about Lazarus (vv. 1-6)

Mary and Martha and their brother Lazarus lived in Bethany, which was very near to Jerusalem. Jesus had a special relationship with this family. The apostle John depicts the closeness of that relationship in two ways. Firstly, he mentions that this is the same Mary who would later anoint the Lord Jesus (12:1-8). Secondly, he explicitly states that Jesus loved each member of this family (v. 5).

Because of the special nature of this relationship, we are not at all surprised to read that Mary and Martha sent a message to Jesus when their brother fell ill. They undoubtedly expected Jesus to come immediately and make Lazarus well, but Jesus delayed for two days (v. 6). The reason he gave for doing so was that Lazarus' sickness was 'not unto death, but for the glory of God, that the Son of God may be glorified through it' (v. 4).

Jesus was not saying that Lazarus would not die but rather that death would not be the final outcome. Do we feel the full force of this? Jesus, who obviously had the power to heal Lazarus, deliberately let him die and allowed his sisters to suffer anguish and pain in order for God to be glorified. (By the way, we should not miss the fact that Jesus clearly identified himself as God.)

Obviously Jesus was concerned about Mary and Martha and how the death of their brother made them feel, but the glory of God was his overriding concern.

- God is worthy of glory (Rom. 11:33-36).

- God specifically created us for his glory (Isa. 43:7; Rev. 4:11).

- Sin means we fall short of the glory of God (Rom. 3:23).

- Those who are redeemed from sin desire God to be glorified (1 Cor. 6:19-20; 10:31; 1 Peter 2:9; 4:11).

'The afflictions of the saints are for the glory of God, that he may have opportunity of showing them favour; for the sweetest mercies, and the most affecting, are those which are occasioned by trouble. Let this reconcile us to the darkest dispensations of Providence, they are all for the glory of God, this sickness, this loss, or this disappointment, is so; and, if God be glorified, we ought to be satisfied'
(Matthew Henry, vol. v, p.1044).

How was God glorified in the death of Lazarus? His resurrection brought:

- many to believe in Jesus (v. 45);

- tremendous blessing to Lazarus and his sisters — all three must have come to greater faith through this experience;

- blessing to the disciples, who also came to greater faith (v. 15);

- the authorities to crucify Jesus, which, in turn, led to incalculable blessing.

Jesus speaks to his disciples (vv. 7-16)

About going to Bethany (vv. 7-10)

When Jesus announced that he was going to Bethany, only two miles from Jerusalem, the disciples were alarmed (v. 8). Jesus responded to their fears with the words of verses 9-10. He affirmed that:

1. the Father had given him a day, an allotment of time, in which to do his work;

2. he was perfectly safe during that time;

3. his business during that time was to walk in the day. Walking in the day refers to submitting to God's will. Walking in the night is refusing to submit.

The same truths apply to us. We each have an allotment of time which cannot be lengthened or shortened. That allotment is sufficient for us to do that which God placed us here to do. Our business is not to worry about the length of our day but rather use it to do God's will.

'...a good man ... relies upon the word of God as his rule, and regards the glory of God as his end, *because he sees* these two great lights, and keeps his eye upon them; thus he is furnished with a faithful guide in all his doubts, and a powerful guard in all his dangers'
(Matthew Henry, vol. v, p.1046, italics are his).

About Lazarus (vv. 11-16)

This conversation, in which Jesus plainly tells his disciples that Lazarus had died, and that he, Jesus, was going to raise him (vv. 11,14), shows us some important spiritual truths.

1. *The glory of the Lord Jesus.* Although he had received no report that Lazarus had died, he knew it.

'...these words respecting Lazarus's sleeping and awaking, express both the omniscience and omnipotence of Christ; his omniscience, that he should know that Lazarus was dead, when at such a distance from him; and his omnipotence, that he could raise him from the dead...'
(John Gill, vol. viii, p.23).

2. *The pleasant way in which Jesus speaks about death* (v. 11). He calls it 'sleep', which implies that it is harmless and temporary for the believer.

' ...why should not the believing hope of ... resurrection to eternal life make it as easy to us to put off the body and die as it is to put off our clothes and go to sleep? ... The grave to the wicked is a prison, and its grave-clothes as the shackles of a criminal reserved for execution; but to the godly it is a bed, and all its bands as the soft and downy fetters of an easy quiet sleep'

(Matthew Henry, vol. v, p.1046).

3. *The glorious hope of believers.* As Jesus promised that he would raise Lazarus from the grave, so he has promised that he will raise to eternal life the bodies of all those who die in faith (14:19).

'We are more sure to arise out of our graves than out of our beds'

(Thomas Watson, cited by I. D. E. Thomas,
A Puritan Golden Treasury, p.246).

4. *The spiritual slowness and dullness of believers.* The disciples did not at first understand that Lazarus had died (v. 12). Then they did not seem to grasp that Jesus was going to raise him. As far as they were concerned, the trip to Bethany would be not to raise Lazarus but to join him (v. 16). We are often like these men. While we have plenty of evidence for the truths of Christianity, we can be fearful, despondent and unbelieving.

DIGGING DEEPER

1. Read verses 1-3. What information do these verses give us about Mary, Martha and Lazarus?

2. *Read verse 4. What was Jesus' explanation for Lazarus' sickness?*

3. *Read verses 5-6. What do these verses tell us about Jesus?*

4. *Read verses 7-10. How did the disciples respond when Jesus decided to return to Judea? How did Jesus respond to their concern?*

5. *Read verses 11-14. How did Jesus view death?*

6. *Read verse 15. What benefit would Lazarus' death achieve for the disciples?*

7. *Read verse 16. How did Thomas respond to Jesus' plan to return to Judea?*

Across:
1. The reason for Lazarus' sickness
5. The town in which Mary, Martha and Lazarus lived
6. He who walks in the night
7. Jesus' word for death

Down:
2. What Jesus felt for Mary, Martha and Lazarus
3. What Thomas expected
4. Didymus

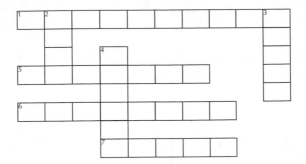

The prelude to Lazarus' resurrection

'Jesus said to her, "I am the resurrection and the life. He who believes in me, though he may die, he shall live"' (v. 25).

The fact that Jesus delayed two days before going to Bethany should not be construed to mean that he was unconcerned and uncaring. The verses of this lesson show us both the reality and the depth of his sympathy for the suffering.

Jesus arrives in Bethany (vv. 17-19)

Upon his arrival Jesus found both hopelessness and helplessness. The hopelessness is forcefully brought home by one phrase: 'he had already been in the tomb four days' (v. 17). The Jews held to the notion that the human spirit hovered around the body for three days to see if it was going to come back to life and could be re-inhabited. On the fourth day, the spirit completely withdrew, and, as far as the Jews were concerned, the situation was irretrievable or irreversible.

The helplessness of the situation comes out in verse 19. There we are told the Jews gathered around Mary and

Martha 'to comfort them concerning their brother'. The Jews could do nothing about the dead. All they could do was to give as much aid as possible to the living.

Jesus ministers to the broken-hearted
(vv. 20-32)

Jesus and Martha (vv. 20-27)

It is apparent from verses 20-24 that the darkness of grief and the light of hope were locked in deadly combat in Martha's heart. At one moment she expressed despair, the next moment she expressed optimism. On one hand, she knew Jesus could have prevented Lazarus from dying and she wondered why he had not come. On the other, she was consoled by the fact that her brother would ultimately rise from the dead. Every believer who has ever had death invade his circle of family or friends has all the commentary he needs on what Martha was going through.

Death reigns like a tyrant over the human race. A reign is composed of an inauguration and an administration. Death was inaugurated when sin came into the human race. Since its inauguration death has carried out a threefold administration:

Physically — the soul is separated from the body
Spiritually — the soul is separated from God
Eternally   — body and soul are separated from God for ever.

In the face of the terrible tyranny of death, Jesus claimed to be the resurrection and the life. These words, the fifth of his 'I am' sayings (v. 25), have brought much comfort to the aching hearts of believers who have lost Christian loved ones. Millions of Christians have walked from cemeteries with the words 'I am the resurrection and the life' echoing in their ears.

Jesus was claiming authority over each aspect of the reign of death. He pulls the sting of physical death by promising to raise the body from the grave (v. 25). He reverses spiritual death by granting spiritual life ('whoever ... lives in me' — v. 26), and he guarantees that those who know him as Lord and Saviour will never die eternally (v. 26).

It must be noted that these promises have a condition attached. They apply only to those who believe in Jesus. Martha believed (v. 27).

'The root of a happy religion is clear, distinct, well-defined knowledge of Jesus Christ'

(J. C. Ryle, *Thoughts*, vol. 2, p.290).

Jesus and Mary (vv. 28-32)

While Jesus was talking with Martha, Mary was sitting in the house (v. 20). The fact that Jesus called for her (v. 28) indicates the tender, personal concern he has for his people.

Mary responded to this by going to Jesus and falling at his feet (vv. 29,31). We find Mary at Jesus' feet on three occasions. In Luke 10:39, she listened to his teaching. Here she craved his sympathy. In John 12:1-8, she anointed him. In each of these instances, she responded to one of Jesus' offices. In the first, she listened to him as prophet. In the second, she sought him as her priest (Heb. 4:15), in the third she anointed him as her king.

We bow before Jesus as prophet when we study his word, as priest when we bring our needs to him and as king when we submit to his rule.

Jesus groans and weeps (vv. 33-37)

The word 'groaned' (v. 33) comes from a Greek word which depicts a stallion rearing, pawing the air and snorting. The word 'troubled' (v. 33) comes from a Greek word which means 'to stir up'. The word 'wept' (v. 35) translates a word which means 'shed tears'. It is not the same weeping as we find in verses 31 and 33, which involved loud expressions of grief.

Why did Jesus weep and feel troubled when he knew that Lazarus would soon be standing beside him in hale and hearty condition? It was due to the utter revulsion he, Jesus, felt towards the ugliness of sin and the damage it creates.

> 'He was moved deeply in the sense of a furious inner anger. Entering His Father's world as the Son of God, He found not order, beauty, harmony, and fulfilment, but fractured disorder, raw ugliness, complete disarray — everywhere the abortion of God's original plan'
>
> (Os Guinness, *Dust of Death*, p.385).

Jesus was sorrowing over:

> '...the awesome dichotomy between what God made and meant man to be and what man had made and marred the situation into being'
>
> (Os Guinness, p.385).

Jesus' sorrow should make us ask if we feel any outrage, any indignation, as we walk through this world. If we are like him, we must. How sad it is that so many of his people often seem to feel at home in this dark, perverted world!

We must also take note that while Jesus was angry at sin, he was not angry at himself. This indicates that God is not responsible for sin and all the heartache it causes.

DIGGING DEEPER

1. *Read verses 17-19. What information do these verses give us about what Jesus found on his arrival in Bethany?*

2. *Read verses 20-27. What did Martha know and believe?*

3. *Read verses 25-26. What do you understand Jesus to be saying in these verses?*

4. *Read verses 28-32. What do you conclude from Jesus calling for Mary? What do these verses tell us about Mary?*

5. *Read verses 33-37. What insights about Jesus do these verses provide?*

Unscramble the following to find a statement made by J. C. Ryle about showing sympathy to others in their times of need:

eno   crsete   fo   gineb   ppyah   si   ot   ryt   ot   keam

___ _____ __ _____ _____ __ __ ___ __ _____

thrseo   hpyap

_____ _____

(J. C. Ryle, vol. 2, p.303).

Jesus raises Lazarus from the dead

'Now when he had said these things, he cried with a loud voice, "Lazarus, come forth!"' (v. 43).

With this passage we come to the last of Jesus' seven signs reported by this Gospel. The significance John attached to this particular sign is reflected by the amount of space he devoted to it. This sign was to him the key element in moving the religious leaders to take action against Jesus and to do so at the precise time ordained by God.

Jesus removes the stone (v. 38)

Two types of caves were used for burial in those days. One, like the tomb in which Jesus himself would be buried, could be characterized as the 'walk-in' variety. A large stone was rolled across the opening. The second was the sloping descent type with a stone laid on the opening. In each case the stone was extremely heavy.

It is interesting that Jesus commanded others to remove the stone. He could have done it himself with a single word, but he uses others to do it. Men can move stones. They cannot raise the dead.

Jesus reassures Martha (vv. 39-40)

Martha's faith reached a pinnacle when she dared to believe that Jesus could raise her brother (v. 22), but here it hits rock bottom. Lazarus had been dead four days, and this made the situation impossible in her eyes. We know about the weakness of faith and how it can waver and vacillate. But the fact that faith is often weak does not mean it is not real. Weak faith is still faith!

How tender and sympathetic Jesus was with Martha! He propped up her weak faith by reminding her of the promise that he had made regarding this situation (v. 4). This reminds us that a good way to treat shaky faith is to take it to the promises of God and to the many times in which God demonstrated his faithfulness to his promises.

Jesus communes with the Father (vv. 41-42)

After speaking to Martha, Jesus spoke to the Father. If Jesus found it necessary to pray, how much more should we! His words were spoken loudly enough (v. 42) to let those around him know that what he was about to do was in conjunction with God and in complete dependence on him. In other words, Jesus framed his action in terms of the issue between himself and the religious leaders, namely, whether he was equal with God.

Jesus cries to Lazarus (vv. 43-44)

The Greek word for 'cried' is used only here in connection with the Lord, and it signifies a very loud, piercing cry. Our Lord obviously intended for all those around to know exactly what was taking place.

The greatness of the Lord's power is brought out in two ways. Firstly, it revived Lazarus. As powerful as death is, it was unable to retain Lazarus in its grip. Secondly, it carried Lazarus out of the tomb. We usually picture Lazarus walking out of the tomb in response to Jesus' cry, but the fact that he was still 'bound hand and foot' when he came out indicates that he was carried out of the tomb by the power of the Lord Jesus.

'Lazarus is a living parable of what Jesus will do, irreversibly, for all believers in the resurrection in the last day, as a result of his own death and resurrection'
(Gordon J. Keddie, vol. 1, p.422).

In relating this miracle, the Holy Spirit refused to supply answers to many of our questions. Where was Lazarus' soul while his body was in the grave? Was it not unkindness to bring him back? Did Lazarus know where his soul had been and could he give an account of it? We must assume that such questions are not answered because God wants us to concentrate on the power and glory that the Lord Jesus demonstrated in raising Lazarus.

The religious leaders confer (vv. 45-57)

This miracle sent shock waves through the religious leaders. It is interesting that they did not try to deny it had taken place (v. 47). There could be no doubt about that because it was performed in the presence of many witnesses (v. 19). But the religious leaders, so firmly in the clutches of hatred for Jesus and so deeply concerned about protecting their own positions of influence, were blind to the clear implications of the miracle.

Jesus divided men in everything he said and did. One would think there could be no division after such a grand display, that all would be forced to admit Jesus was nothing less than God in human flesh and would have to bow before him in submission and faith. Some did (v. 45). But others were so hard in their hearts that this event only caused them to hate him more intensely and made them more determined to eliminate him (v. 53). We should not be surprised at this because we still see Jesus dividing people into the same camps of believers and unbelievers.

The words of Caiaphas the high priest are of special interest (vv. 49-50). While speaking freely from the wickedness of his heart, he uttered the truth of the gospel. He and the other leaders were concerned that the people would soon accept Jesus as the Messiah, which would cause the Romans to assume that he, Jesus, would lead a rebellion against them. To prevent this, they would march against the Jews and put many of them to death. Caiaphas reasoned, therefore, that it was necessary to immediately put one person to death — Jesus!

The gospel message is in these words. Jesus was put to death on the cross, bearing the wrath of God there, so that all who believe in him will not have to endure that wrath themselves.

'Let us turn from the whole passage with thoughts of comfort and consolation. Comfortable is the thought that the loving Saviour of sinners, on whose mercy our souls entirely depend, is one who has all power in heaven and earth, and is mighty to save — Comfortable is the thought that there is no sinner too far gone in sin for Christ to raise and convert. He that stood by the grave of Lazarus can say to the vilest of men, "Come forth: loose him, and let him go." — Comfortable, not least, is the thought that when we ourselves lie down in the grave, we may lie down in the full assurance that we shall rise again. The voice that called Lazarus forth will one day pierce our tombs, and bid soul and body come together'

(J. C. Ryle, vol. 2, p.318).

'What Caiaphas said was true, of course, but not as he meant it. His spirit was hostile to Christ and yet the Holy Spirit was at work here. The high priest, Caiaphas, in spite of himself, became a prophet. For it was indeed true that Christ would die for the salvation of the people'

(S. G. DeGraaf, vol. iv, p.78).

DIGGING DEEPER

1. *Read verses 38-40. What was Martha's objection? How did Jesus respond to it?*

2. *Read verses 41-42. Why did Jesus pray on this occasion?*

3. *Read verses 43-44. What do these verses tell us about the Lord Jesus Christ?*

4. *Read verses 45-48. How did the religious leaders respond to the resurrection of Lazarus? Why did they fear Jesus?*

5. *Read verses 49-53. How did Caiaphas view the situation? How did the apostle John view his words?*

6. *Read verses 54-57. Where did Jesus go after leaving Bethany? What feast was near? What were the religious leaders planning to do with Jesus at the feast?*

Read Luke 7:11-17 and 8:40-42,49-56 for the two other instances in which Jesus raised someone from the dead. Answer the following questions:

                    Luke 7:11-17   Luke 8:40-42,49-56

Who was raised?   _____   _____

Where did this happen?   _____   _____

What did Jesus say? _____   _____

                     _____   _____

WEEK 32
John 12:1-11

The anointing at Bethany

 'Then Mary took a pound of very costly oil of spikenard, anointed the feet of Jesus, and wiped his feet with her hair. And the house was filled with the fragrance of the oil' (v. 3).

In these verses, the apostle John takes us from one extreme to the other. On one hand, we have Mary's anointing of Jesus, one of the most warm and tender events imaginable. On the other hand, in the plotting of the religious leaders to kill Lazarus (and, of course, Jesus), we are taken to the extreme of cruel hatred.

The worshipping of Mary (vv. 1-8)

The anointing of Jesus by Mary occurred in Bethany at the house of Simon the leper (Matt. 26:6). Simon evidently hosted a supper for Jesus to thank him for healing him of his leprosy. He also invited Mary, Martha and Lazarus to join them. Because Jesus had raised him from the dead only a few days earlier, Lazarus and his sisters would have welcomed the opportunity to share in honouring Jesus. It appears that Lazarus was also an honoured guest (v. 2).

Martha was again busy serving (v. 2), but probably without the anxiety and distraction of a former time (Luke 10:38). Mary was again at Jesus' feet.

'She sat at *His feet* when the sun was shining. Then when the
darkness was round about her, and Lazarus was dead, and
her heart was breaking, she came when He sent for her, and
went straight to *His feet*. Now it was His day of approaching
sorrow, and again she went straight to *His feet'*
(G. Campbell Morgan, *The Gospel According to John*,
p.207, italics are his).

On this occasion Mary anointed Jesus' head (Matt. 26:7)
and his feet with an ointment that was, according to Judas'
assessment, worth three hundred denarii (v. 5), nearly a
year's wages. Mary gave this gift in a free and uninhibited
fashion, that is, without regard to the conventions of the
day. It was considered indecent for a woman to loose her
hair in public. But Mary's love for Jesus was such that she
did not let either the costliness of the gift or the customs of
the day stop her.

What prompted Mary's act (vv. 1-3)

1. *Love.*

'Those who love Christ truly love him so much better than
this world as to lay out the best they have for him'
(Matthew Henry, vol. v, p.1068).

2. *Gratitude.* Mary had many, many reasons to be grateful
to Jesus. He had been in her home several times. He had
instructed her and her family in the things of God. When
Lazarus died, Jesus had spoken words of comfort and hope
(11:25-26) and had raised him from the dead. All of these
things must have gone racing through Mary's mind on this
occasion.

3. *Understanding.* Mary did not just 'happen' to have the costly ointment on hand. She had deliberately purchased it for the day of Jesus' burial (v. 7). Jesus had often predicted his death at the hand of his enemies, but only Mary seemed to really understand.

> 'Mary was, perhaps, the best listener Jesus ever had'
> (William Hendriksen, p.180).

Mary had brought the ointment with her to Simon's house. She must have realized that Jesus' death was very near and that there was a strong possibility that his enemies would not allow her to anoint his body for burial. She determined, therefore, that she would anoint him while she had the opportunity.

What Mary's act prompted (vv. 4-8)

1. *Criticism from Judas and the other disciples* (vv. 4-6). Mary's action touched off a wave of criticism. Judas claimed to be outraged over the 'waste' of the ointment. He argued that it should have been sold and the proceeds given to the poor.

Judas' indignation was due to him seeing a missed opportunity. If Mary had decided to give the ointment to the poor, she would almost certainly have asked Jesus to help her, and Jesus would have asked Judas, the treasurer for the disciples, to sell the ointment. Judas would then have been able to pocket the proceeds. John puts it plainly: 'This he said, not that he cared for the poor, but because he was a thief, and had the money box; and he used to take what was put in it' (v. 6).

John makes no mention of this, but Matthew and Mark tell us that the other disciples agreed with Judas. Matthew

says they were 'indignant' (Matt. 26:8-9), and Mark says
they 'criticized her sharply' (Mark 14:5).

> 'A cold heart and a stingy hand will generally go together'
>   (J. C. Ryle, vol. 2, p.349).

2. *Commendation from Jesus* (vv. 7-8). Jesus immediately
came to Mary's defence on two fronts. He first informed the
disciples that Mary had heard what they had failed to hear,
that is, that he would soon die. With this in mind she had
anointed him for burial (v. 7).

> 'Our Lord Jesus thought much and often of his own death and
> burial; it would be good for us to do so too'
>   (Matthew Henry, vol. v, pp.1069-70).

Jesus also informed the disciples that the poor would always
be present with them and could be helped by them at any
time, but he would not always be with them in the way he
was then (v. 8). Jesus was not suggesting that his disciples
should neglect the poor. He was calling them to recognize
the uniqueness of that moment. He was urging them to not
let the good, the feeding of the poor, become the enemy of
the best, loving and worshipping him.

> 'That good duty which may be done at *any time* ought to give
> way to that which cannot be done but *just now*'
>   (Matthew Henry, vol. v, p.1070, italics are his).

Mary's act of love offers a mighty challenge to us. She was
essentially saying three things to Jesus:

- I owe you more than I can ever repay.
- I don't care what others might think or say.
- I won't wait to show my love.

The Lord Jesus has certainly been as good to us as he was to Mary. Do we feel the love for him that Mary felt? What are we doing to express that love?

The plotting of the religious leaders (vv. 9-11)

Mary's act of love is set against the backdrop of the religious leaders' continued and increased hatred of Jesus. This hatred even drove them to plan how they could do away with Lazarus. They wanted to remove Lazarus because he was attracting a lot of attention (v. 9) and was causing many to come to faith in Christ (v. 11).

The religious leaders apparently assumed that if Lazarus were to die again, it would in some way diminish his resurrection. It did not seem to occur to them that another death for Lazarus might very well mean another resurrection and only make matters worse!

There is no indication that the plot against Lazarus was carried out. The triumphal entry of Jesus into Jerusalem must have convinced the religious leaders that they had to take action very quickly against Jesus and not concern themselves with Lazarus.

DIGGING  DEEPER

1. Read verses 1-2. When and where did Mary anoint Jesus?

2. Read verse 3. What details does this verse provide?

3. Read verses 4-6. How did Judas respond to Mary's act? How did John explain the response of Judas?

4. Read verse 7. How did Jesus explain Mary's act?

5. Read verse 8. What does this verse teach?

Find and circle in the puzzle below four key words from this week's lesson.

```
F  W  O  I  L  M  K  Z  V  B  P
G  R  N  T  B  O  Q  I  I  E  H
W  E  A  Z  M  A  R  Y  I  T  X
Z  Z  X  G  M  E  R  T  T  H  P
A  A  F  C  R  U  K  O  L  A  N
D  F  G  M  N  A  O  E  I  N  B
J  C  N  E  T  T  N  X  Q  Y  O
V  M  N  C  T  I  W  C  W  U  V
T  F  J  K  L  B  V  C  E  O  E
```

Jesus triumphantly enters Jerusalem

'Fear not, daughter of Zion;
Behold, your King is coming,
Sitting on a donkey's colt' (v. 15).

Jesus' arrival in Jerusalem marks the beginning of what we know as 'Holy Week'. Beginning with Jesus being hailed and acclaimed as King of the Jews, this week ended with him dying in shame and agony on a Roman cross. Perhaps no single week in history produced a greater change. On Sunday the people were waving their palm branches and crying 'Hosanna!' On Friday they were shaking their fists and crying 'Crucify him!'

How are we to explain such a swift and dramatic change? The answer lies in the nature of Jesus' kingdom. When the people thought he was offering a political, temporal kingdom, they hailed him. When they realized that he had no plan to establish such a kingdom, they abandoned him. One of the primary values of this passage, then, is its warning about trying to accept Jesus on our terms.

The multitude (vv. 12-15,17-18)

Excitement about Jesus had been building for a period of several days. As far as many were concerned, his raising of

Lazarus proved that Jesus was their long-awaited Messiah. These people were also convinced that the Passover was the right time for Jesus to claim the throne. What better time for deliverance from Rome than the celebration of their fathers' deliverance from Egypt?

Such thinking led many to monitor Jesus closely. Early on this particular Sunday morning, they went to nearby Bethany where he had been staying. What they saw and heard there convinced them that Jesus was ready to make his move.

Some then ran to Jerusalem to announce the news, and people began to pour out of the city to welcome Jesus. Others accompanied him to Jerusalem. When the two crowds merged, the people began waving branches from the palm trees lining the way, spreading their garments before him (a customary way of greeting a conquering king) and crying 'Hosanna!' ('save now').

Jesus did not share the euphoria of the multitude. Luke's Gospel tells us that he wept as he approached the city (Luke 19:41-44). He, the great discerner of men, knew that this was not true acceptance. The people were hailing him, not for the king he came to be, but rather for the king they wanted him to be. In other words, they were acclaiming him as a temporal, political Messiah who was about to overthrow the Romans and lead Israel back to a position of supremacy among the nations.

The multitude was so caught in the excitement of the moment that the obvious symbolism Jesus had chosen was lost on them. The Messiah they wanted should have been mounted on an impressive stallion, but Jesus came riding on a lowly donkey, a plain declaration that his kingdom would not be set up by political force.

Had the multitude realized this, they would have said, 'This is not our Messiah!' and thrown down their palm branches at once. The problem was not with Jesus. He was indeed their Messiah. It was rather that they had a false expectation of him, an expectation that was born out of a misreading of the prophecies of the Old Testament.

The error of the multitude is still alive. Many accept Jesus as they want him to be rather than as he has declared himself to be.

The disciples (v. 16)

Even Jesus' disciples did not understand until later the significance of Jesus' entry into Jerusalem. After Jesus arose from the dead, they realized that his mode of entry fulfilled the prophecy of Zechariah 9:9.

The fulfilment of prophecy is, of course, one of the major proofs that Jesus was indeed God in human flesh and the Saviour of mankind. One count has Jesus fulfilling approximately 325 prophecies. The mathematical probability of one man fulfilling just a few prophecies is staggering. Peter Stoner writes:

> 'We find that the chance that any man might have lived down to the present time and fulfilled ... eight prophecies is ... 1 in 100,000,000,000,000,000'
>
> (cited by Josh McDowell,
> *The New Evidence That Demands a Verdict*, p.193).

The Pharisees (v. 19)

> 'The *more radical* Pharisees said to the *milder* party — "You see that you are gaining nothing, by your delay. Something has to be done, and done quickly, or it will be too late"'
>
> (William Hendriksen, vol. ii, p.192, italics are his).

Why did Jesus allow himself to be acclaimed as king when he knew the people were thinking of a different kind of king? He was forcing the hand of the religious leaders. The overwhelming enthusiasm of the people convinced them that something had to be done about Jesus and it had to be done quickly. The Pharisees undoubtedly preferred to wait until after the Passover to remove Jesus from the scene.

But Jesus had a different timetable in mind. He was the 'Lamb of God' who had come to take away sin. As God's Lamb, it was essential for him to be sacrificed on the Passover. By evoking this public demonstration, Jesus was forcing the religious leaders to adopt his timetable.

DIGGING DEEPER

1. *Read verses 12-13. What details do these verses provide?*

2. *Read verses 14-15. Why did Jesus choose a donkey on which to ride?*

3. *Read verse 16. What and when did Jesus' disciples understand?*

4. *Read verses 17-18. What part did the resurrection of Lazarus play in the triumphal entry?*

5. *Read verse 19. How did the Pharisees respond?*

Use the first letters of the missing words in the verses below to arrive at one of the key words in this week's lesson:

'But be doers of the word, and not _____ only, deceiving yourselves' (James 1:22).

'But Peter and the other apostles answered and said: "We ought to _____ God rather than men"' (Acts 5:29).

'_____ the LORD with gladness...' (Ps. 100:2).

'For I am not _____ of the gospel of Christ, for it is the power of God to salvation...' (Rom. 1:16).

'...how shall we escape if we _____ so great a salvation...' (Heb. 2:3).

'I will praise your _____ ...' (Isa. 25:1).

'_____ to righteousness, and do not sin...' (1 Cor. 15:34).

KEY WORD: ___ ___ ___ ___ ___ ___ ___

The aftermath of the Greeks' request

'If anyone serves me, let him follow me; and where I am, there my servant will be also. If anyone serves me, him my Father will honour' (v. 26).

Gentiles who had embraced the Jewish religion came to Jerusalem to observe the Passover. Included among these were the Greeks to whom these verses refer. These men apparently had a deep, inner longing that had never been satisfied. Failing to find fulfilment in the many gods of Greek culture, they had turned to the monotheism of the Jews, but it had not been able to completely satisfy the longing of their hearts.

The news they had heard about Jesus encouraged them to believe that he could help them. They approached Philip (perhaps because of his Greek name) to see if he would arrange a meeting with Jesus (vv. 20-21). Philip approached Andrew with their request, who joined him in taking it to Jesus (v. 22).

Jesus speaks with Andrew and Philip (vv. 23-26)

Jesus did not consent to a meeting with these men. He evidently intended for Andrew and Philip to convey his message to them — the message of the cross. He wanted the Greeks to understand that the satisfaction for which they yearned could only be supplied by his death. He wanted them to see what the multitude (vv. 12-19) had failed to see, namely, that his kingdom was spiritual in nature.

Notice the following about Jesus' forthcoming death:

- It was the 'hour' for which he had come to this world (v. 23).
- That shameful death would be the means of bringing glory to Jesus (v. 23). Through that death he would provide eternal salvation.
- It was absolutely necessary to produce spiritual life (v. 24).
- It would set a pattern for his people to follow (vv. 25-26).

Jesus speaks to the Father (vv. 27-28)

While Jesus constantly felt the need to pray, he never seemed to feel it more than when he contemplated his forthcoming death on the cross. The thought of that cross caused him to be 'troubled' in his soul (v. 27).

Why was Jesus troubled? For him death on the cross would mean enduring the wrath of God!

'The horror of paying the wages of sin sinks in and troubles his innermost being. His true humanity shrinks from death, as we all instinctively do, but the heart of the incarnate Son of God contemplates with trembling the prospect of the wrath of the Father against sin not his own. Here is a foretaste of Gethsemane…'

(Gordon J. Keddie, vol. 1, p.471).

'Nothing can ever explain our Lord's trouble of soul, both here and in Gethsemane, except the old doctrine, that He felt the burden of man's sin pressing Him down. It was the mighty weight of a world's guilt imputed to Him and meeting on his head, which made Him groan and agonise, and cry, "Now is my soul troubled." For ever let us cling to that doctrine, not only as untying the knot of the passage before us, but as the only ground of solid comfort for the heart of a Christian. That our sins have been really laid on our divine Substitute, and borne by Him, and that His righteousness is really imputed to us and accounted ours — this is the real warrant for Christian peace'

(J. C. Ryle, vol. 2, pp.387-8).

The fact that Jesus was troubled tells us something about the tremendous cost he paid for the salvation of his people.

The Father speaks from heaven (v. 28)

The fact that the Father spoke so quickly from heaven confirmed his love for his Son and gave indisputable proof of the divine nature of Jesus, as it did on two previous occasions (see Matt. 3:17; 17:5). The Father's response also proved that he and Jesus were 'of one mind' regarding the cross. Jesus would go to the cross to glorify the name of the Father, and the Father, who had glorified his name in the past, would glorify it again through Jesus' death.

How did the cross glorify the name of the Father? It showed God to be just (because sin was punished there), gracious (because it provided salvation for sinners), wise (because it satisfied the demands of justice and grace), and faithful (because it fulfilled the promises of God).

Jesus speaks with the people (vv. 29-36)

The people were confused by the sound of the voice. Some thought it had only thundered, while others thought an angel had spoken (v. 29). People are still attributing to angels that which belongs to God alone!

The Lord Jesus responded to their confusion by pointing out the following:

- The voice had not come exclusively for his sake, but also for theirs (v. 30).

- The voice signified the greatness of what he would accomplish on the cross — nothing less than the defeat of Satan himself! (v. 31). The cross would shatter the power of Satan to keep the nations (represented by the Greeks) in darkness. The cross would also be the means of drawing people to salvation even as a magnet draws iron.

It is striking that Jesus kept the focus on his death and not on the voice. How easy it is to be more interested in the sensational than in the truth!

But the people were not interested in a crucified Messiah. They assumed that the Messiah would remain on earth for ever as the ruler of the Jews (v. 34). This notion showed the spiritual darkness of these people, darkness that could only be driven away by the light of Christ (vv. 35-36).

DIGGING DEEPER

1. *Read verses 20-22. How did the request of the Greeks get to Jesus?*

2. *Read verses 23-26. What do these verses tell us about the cross of Christ?*

3. *Read verses 27-28. What did Jesus ask the Father to do regarding his forthcoming death? How did the Father respond?*

4. *Read verse 29. How did the people respond to the Father's voice?*

5. *Read verses 30-32. What additional information about the cross do these verses provide?*

6. *Read verses 33-34. How did the people respond to the idea of a crucified Messiah?*

7. *Read verses 35-36. What do you understand from these verses?*

Fill in the missing words. Use the first letter of each of the missing words to arrive at the key word.

'And the God of peace will _____ Satan under your feet shortly' (Rom. 16:20).

'in whom we have _____ through his blood, the forgiveness of sins' (Col. 1:14).

'And being found in appearance as a man, he humbled himself and became _____ to the point of death, even the death of the cross' (Phil. 2:8).

'And my _____ has rejoiced in God my _____' (Luke 1:47).

KEY WORD: ___ ___ ___ ___ ___

A summary of Jesus' public ministry

'I have come as a light into the world, that whoever believes in me should not abide in darkness' (v. 46).

The apostle John completed his description of the public ministry of Jesus in verse 36. Before turning to the private ministry of Jesus (conducted among the twelve), John gives us a summary of Jesus' public ministry. This summary consists of two parts: an explanation of unbelief (vv. 37-43) and a call to faith (vv. 44-50).

An explanation of unbelief (vv. 37-43)

While many believed in Jesus during his public ministry, the vast majority of the people and the religious leaders rejected him (1:11-12). In these verses, the apostle John dwells on various aspects of this rejection.

The surprising nature of it (v. 37)

The rejection of Jesus would have been understandable had he merely stated his claims and nothing else. But Jesus had substantiated his claims with 'many signs'. And these signs were not done in a corner. They were 'before them', that is, before the very ones who rejected Jesus. In summary, we can say that the miracles of Jesus were many in number, convincing in nature and public in presentation. But Jesus was still rejected.

The unsurprising nature of it (v. 38)

In another way, the rejection of Jesus was not surprising at all. It was prophesied centuries before! (Isa. 53:1).

'The arm of the LORD' had been revealed in the miracles that Jesus performed, but the people 'could not believe' (v. 39) because their eyes were blinded and their hearts were hardened (v. 40), as Isaiah had prophesied (Isa. 6:9-10).

> 'In order that the divine moral order, as decreed from eternity and as described by the prophets, might be fulfilled, the Jewish multitudes, *through their own fault*, failed to accept Christ by genuine faith. That divine order demands that those who wilfully harden themselves shall be hardened. When Pharaoh hardens his heart, God carries out his plan (Rom. 9:17) with respect to him, and hardens his heart even more … *the fault lies not in any sense with God*! He is the God of love. He is not a cruel monster who deliberately and with inward delight prepares people for everlasting damnation. On the contrary, he earnestly warns, proclaims the Gospel, and states — as Jesus did repeatedly during his earthly ministry — what will happen if people believe, also what will happen if they do not. He even *urges* them to walk in the light. But when people, of their own accord and after repeated threats and promises, reject him and spurn his messages, then — and not until then — he hardens them, *in order that* those who were *not willing* to repent may *not be able* to repent'
>
> (William Hendriksen, vol. ii, pp.211-2, italics are his).

A call to faith (vv. 44-50)

In these verses, John apparently draws on statements that Jesus made at various times throughout his ministry to create a summary of its main themes.

Jesus is one with God and the way to God (vv. 44-45)

The one who believes in Jesus does not believe in Jesus alone because Jesus was both God and sent by God (v. 44). To see Jesus was, then, to see God (v. 45). This constitutes an unanswerable proof for the existence of God. Do we see in the life of Jesus evidence that he was God in human flesh? If so, we have to say God exists!

Other references: 7:16; 8:19,42; 10:30,38.

Jesus is the light of the world (v. 46)

Each inhabitant of this world has been darkened by sin. It is not a matter of us being in the darkness. It is rather that the darkness is in us. Our minds are so darkened that we cannot comprehend the truth of God. Our hearts are so darkened that we do not love God. Our wills are so darkened that we do not seek God. As the light, Jesus gives light in each of these areas.

Other references: 1:4-5,9; 8:12; 9:5; 12:35-36.

Jesus did not come to judge but to save (vv. 47-48)

Jesus was simply saying that his primary purpose in coming to this world was not to exercise judgement but to provide salvation. Of course, this must not be taken to mean that there will be no judgement for unbelievers. There will be a day of judgement, on which the words of Jesus will be the standard for passing sentence. Did Jesus say that believers will be saved and unbelievers will perish? On Judgement Day, all will be reminded of that word, and no one will be able to deny it.

> 'Do you think that this world will continue indefinitely? A person has a right to his opinion, I suppose. But I prefer the word of the Lord Jesus Christ who said that all things will not continue as they are, that a future day of judgement is coming, and that all men and women will in that day have to answer for what they have said and done'
>
> (James Montgomery Boice, p.861).

Other references: 3:17; 5:24,45-47; 8:15-16,31,37,51.

The words Jesus spoke are the words of the Father (v. 49)

This is yet another dimension to his oneness with the Father. Jesus spoke the words of the Father, with the authority of the Father.

Other references: 3:11; 7:16; 8:26,28,38.

The words of the Father are the words of life (v. 50)

Eternal life is found in heeding the words that the Lord Jesus spoke.

Other references: 3:16; 6:63.

DIGGING DEEPER

1. *Read verses 37-41. What explanation do these verses give for people rejecting Jesus?*

2. *Read verses 42-43. What reason do these verses give for rejection of Jesus?*

3. *Read verses 44-45. What do these verses teach about Jesus' relationship with the Father?*

4. *Read verse 46. What does Jesus promise here?*

5. *Read verses 47-49. What do these verses teach about judgement?*

6. *Read verse 50. What does this verse teach about the nature of the Word of God and about Jesus' commitment to it?*

Look up the following verses about the cross of Christ. In the blanks provided write the attribute of God that is glorified by the cross:

1 Corinthians 1:18   _____

1 Corinthians 1:21-25   _____

Romans 3:25-26   _____

Hebrews 2:9   _____

Acts 13:23   _____

Two demonstrations of humility

'If I then, your Lord and Teacher, have washed your feet, you also ought to wash one another's feet' (13:14).

With this lesson we come to a major transition in John's Gospel. Chapters 1-12 deal with the public ministry of Jesus, but these verses turn our attention to the ministry of Jesus to his disciples (13:1 - 17:26). The rest of the Gospel is taken up with John's account of Gethsemane, the crucifixion and the resurrection.

The supper described in these verses took place the night before Jesus was crucified. Jesus used this time to demonstrate humility to his disciples.

Jesus washes the feet of his disciples (vv. 1-17)

The reason for Jesus' humble service (vv. 1-5)

Why did Jesus wash the disciples' feet? Their feet were dirty! The streets and roads of that day were so dusty that the feet became unclean when walking even a short distance. It was customary, therefore, for a host to provide for the rinsing of the feet when guests arrived. This was normally the job of one of the household servants.

Jesus and his disciples apparently rented this room for their supper with the understanding that there would be no host or servant there. The owner of the room made sure the water and the basin for rinsing were present, but no one was there to wash the feet. In such a situation, the task fell to the person of lowest status. However, none of the disciples was willing to admit that he was beneath the others. Indeed, they would argue that very evening about 'which of them should be considered the greatest' (Luke 22:24). It is not surprising, then, that they all walked right past the water and the basin and took their places at the table.

They must have been shocked at what happened next. Jesus suddenly rose from his place and began the menial task. The greatest among them was willing to do the work of the lowest!

'The very act of washing his disciples' feet was to be a picture of that voluntary humiliation whereby he had laid aside his "existence-form as God", had assumed the garment of human flesh, had taken the place of a servant, had even stooped to the death of the cross, that he might cleanse his followers from sin'

(Charles R. Erdman, p.121).

A response to Jesus' humble service (vv. 6-11)

Simon Peter strenuously objected to Jesus washing his feet. We may picture him drawing them up as he says, 'You shall never wash my feet!' (v. 8). Jesus' response was: 'If I do not wash you, you have no part with me.' If Peter could not accept Jesus' humiliation on his behalf at this point, he would not be able to share in the redemption that would only be provided through Jesus' complete humiliation on the cross.

'In making this protest Peter was in fact displaying the pride of unredeemed men and women, who are so confident of their ability to save themselves that they instinctively resist the suggestion that they need divine cleansing. They desire to do everything for themselves'

(R. V. G. Tasker, *The Gospel According to St John*, p.155).

Peter then went to the opposite extreme and asked Jesus to give him a bath. But Jesus pointed out that he only needed to have his feet washed. Peter may not have realized it, but Jesus here articulated vital teaching. The Christian gets a once-for-all bath when he is saved. After that he never again needs a bath, but he does need to have his feet cleansed on a daily basis. Although the Christian is saved for ever, he still becomes contaminated by sin as he walks through this world. He does not need to be saved again, but he does need to confess and be cleansed of those sins he commits.

The application of Jesus' humble service (vv. 14-17)

If the one they called 'Lord' and 'Master' had been willing to stoop in menial service, the disciples should be willing to serve others. Some have taken these verses to mean that churches should conduct foot-washing, but that misses the point. Jesus washed the disciples' feet to meet a real need. Their feet were dirty. We do not follow his example by meeting in our churches to wash feet that are already clean, but rather by helping our brothers and sisters in Christ with their needs.

Jesus gives Judas a morsel of food (vv. 18-30)

Jesus' washing of the disciples' feet was certainly an act of great humility, but it is not the only act of humility in this lesson. How Jesus responded to Judas also demonstrated his humility.

Jesus knew in advance that Judas was going to hand him over to his enemies. He had spoken of this on a previous occasion (John 6:71), and he spoke of it again after returning to his place at the table (v. 21).

This statement led, of course, to an immediate inquiry about who would do such a thing. The fact that many of the disciples did not seem to pick up on the fact that Jesus identified the traitor (v. 28) indicates that they fell to discussing it among themselves and were distracted while only Peter and John saw and understood the identification (vv. 24-26).

Some see Jesus' handing the morsel of food to Judas as a token of friendship and a final plea to him to turn from his plans. Others see it only as Jesus' way of answering John's question. This much is apparent — Jesus could have stopped Judas from betraying him, but he knew the betrayal was part of the course the Father had laid out for him and he refused to stop it. Instead he submitted to the will of his Father.

William Hendriksen writes of Jesus:

'He had seen the coming of the storm but instead of avoiding it he had walked right into it'

(vol. ii, p.251).

It is no wonder that Jesus said immediately after Judas left that God was 'glorified' (v. 31). God is always glorified when his will is obeyed.

DIGGING   DEEPER

1. *Read verse 1. When did the events John is about to describe take place? To what event does 'the hour' refer? What does this verse teach about the love of Jesus?*

2. *Read verses 2-5. What further information do these verses give?*

3. *Read verses 6-11. Why do you think Simon did not want Jesus to wash his feet? What spiritual principles did Jesus teach him?*

4. *Read verses 12-17. What are some ways in which we can do as Jesus did on this occasion? Why should we do such things?*

5. *Read verses 18-20. Why did Jesus forewarn the disciples about his betrayal? What does Jesus claim in verse 20?*

6. *Read verses 21-30. How did Jesus identify Judas as his betrayer? Why did this not register with the other disciples?*

Jesus took seven distinct steps in washing the disciples' feet, each of which pictures some aspect of redemption. Identify these pictures by filling in the blanks.

1. As Jesus rose from his place at supper, so he rose from his place in _____ (John 3:31).

2. As Jesus laid aside his garments, so he laid aside his _____ (John 17:5).

3. As Jesus girded himself with a towel, so he girded himself with our _____ (John 1:14).

4. As he poured the water into the basin, so he poured out his _____ (Rev. 1:5) on the _____ (Col. 1:20).

5. As he cleansed their feet from defilement, so he has cleansed believers from the defilement of _____ (Rev. 1:5).

6. As he put on his garments again, so he has taken his _____ again (Luke 24:46; 1 Tim. 3:16).

7. As he sat down (v. 12), so he has sat down at the _____ _____ of God (Heb. 1:3).

Jesus prepares his disciples for his departure

'Jesus said to him, "I am the way, the truth, and the life. No one comes to the Father except through me"' (14:6).

The storm clouds of the cross have gathered around Jesus and are about to break with fury upon him. The 'hour' is now only hours away. Jesus is with his disciples. Supper is over and the traitor, Judas Iscariot, has departed to perform his black deed. Only Jesus' 'little children' are left (13:33). The next night at this time his body would be lying in a dark, cool tomb, and the disciples would be crushed and confused.

This passage gives us some of the words that Jesus spoke to his disciples in those precious moments they had together.

A new commandment (13:33-35)

Jesus prefaced his command with the announcement that he would only be with the disciples 'a little while longer', that he was about to do what he had come to do; that is, glorify God through his death (vv. 31-32).

The need for love (v. 34)

Why would he mention this immediately before commanding them to love each other? Was he telling them that they would need to draw strength from each other now that they would be without his physical presence? They would not be able to do this if they were at odds with each other.

The measure of love

Jesus called his command to love 'a new commandment'. But God's people have been responsible to love each other from early times (Lev. 19:18). The thing that makes this commandment new is that Jesus gave a new standard or measurement for love. The disciples were to love each other even as he had loved them. We might say, therefore, that Jesus was giving an old command new force and new meaning.

How had Jesus loved them? That very night he had washed their feet. The next day he was going to die on the cross. The love of Jesus was, therefore, manifested in concrete acts of sacrificial service. We need to reflect long and hard on this. We have a tendency to equate love with a warm, affable feeling for others, but true love manifests itself. It is, of course, impossible for us to completely love as Jesus did, but we ought to be striving towards the standard he set.

The result of love (v. 35)

The kind of love Jesus commanded cannot go unnoticed by the people of the world. This type of love convinces unbelievers that there is something to Christianity. All too often we undermine what we say about Christianity by reflecting bitterness, resentment and dissension.

'It is called a "new" commandment, not because it had never been given before, but because it was to be more honoured, to occupy a higher position, to be backed by a higher example than it ever had been before. Above all, it was to be the test of Christianity before the world …

'Let us take heed that this well-known Christian grace is not merely a notion in our heads, but a practice in our lives. Of all the commands of our Master there is none which is so much talked about and so little obeyed as this. Yet, if we mean anything when we profess to have charity and love toward all men, it ought to be seen in our tempers and our words, our bearing and our doing, our behaviour at home and abroad, our conduct in every relation of life. Specially it ought to show itself forth in all our dealing with other Christians'

(J. C. Ryle, vol. 3, pp.46-7).

A shocking prediction (13:36-38)

Jesus' words about his departure prompted Simon Peter to ask where he was going (v. 36). Jesus was, of course, going to his death on the cross. Simon's time would come! (v. 36). Much too sure of himself, Simon assured the Lord that he was not only willing to follow him at that very moment but also to lay down his life for him (v. 37). How shocking it was for him to hear Jesus predict that he, Simon, would deny him three times that very night! (v. 38). This prediction came true, proving again that Jesus was God in human flesh.

'Let it be a settled principle in our religion, that there is an amount of weakness in all our hearts, of which we have no adequate conception, and that we never know how far we might fall if we were tempted'

(J. C. Ryle, vol. 3, pp.47-8).

A comforting promise (14:1-6)

The disciples certainly had much over which to be despondent on this night. The cure for despondency is faith. And this is exactly what Jesus called them to. He says, '... you believe in God, believe also in me' (v. 1). Some translate this phrase, '...believe in God, believe also in me'.

It appears to have been a strange thing for Jesus to say. The disciples already believed in both God and himself. Why, then, did Jesus urge them to believe in something they already believed in? The answer lies in the nature of faith. Faith consists of degrees, and Jesus was calling them to believe more completely than they had ever done so before.

He then proceeded to give some specific truths for his disciples to embrace more fully.

He was going away to prepare a place for them

What a wonderful term he uses for heaven! He calls it 'my Father's house'. This implies that it is a place of plentiful provision, unfailing protection, delight and pleasure. But heaven is not such a place that sinners can casually stroll into. It is a prepared place for a prepared people. Jesus made all the necessary preparations for heaven to receive sinners by dying on the cross.

Jesus gave his disciples reason to believe this promise by assuring them of the reliability of his word. We often decide about the reliability of information we receive by considering the nature of the person who gives us that information. Jesus rested his promises squarely on himself, saying, '...if it were not so, I would have told you' (v. 2).

He would come again to receive them unto himself (v. 3)

It is interesting that Jesus did not say he would come again to take them to that place. That would have been true. But Jesus said he would receive them unto himself. This shows us that the true treasure of heaven is the Lord Jesus himself.

This section closes with the sixth of Jesus' 'I am' sayings (v. 6). Jesus is the way to the heaven of which he spoke by virtue of being the truth and the life. In other words, he is the way to heaven because he enlightens our minds to understand the truth and because he grants spiritual life to us.

'How much they possess who live the life of faith in the Son of God, and believe in Jesus! With all their weaknesses and crosses they have that which the world can neither give nor take away. They have a true Friend while they live, and a true home when they die'

(J. C. Ryle, vol. 3, p.59).

DIGGING DEEPER

1. Read 13:31-33. To what event is Jesus referring in these verses? What would this event accomplish?

2. Read 13:34-35. Why is this command new? What does obedience to this command accomplish?

3. Read 13:36-38. What lesson should we draw for ourselves from Simon Peter's words? What do these verses teach us about Jesus?

4. *Read 14:1. What does Jesus propose for troubled hearts?*

5. *Read 14:2-3. What does Jesus promise in these verses?*

6. *Read 14:4-6. How is Jesus the way to heaven?*

The words 'love one another' represent one of many responsibilities that Christians have to 'one another'. Using the verses on the left, write in the blanks provided some other responsibilities:

Romans 14:13 _____

Romans 15:7 _____

Galatians 6:2 _____

Ephesians 4:2 _____

Ephesians 4:32 _____

1 Thessalonians 5:11 _____

Hebrews 10:24 _____

James 4:11 _____

James 5:16 _____

James 5:16 _____

Four reasons for comfort

'If you love me, keep my commandments'
(14:15).

These verses contain words Jesus spoke to his disciples on the night before he was crucified. Knowing their sorrow over his impending departure, Jesus gave them words of comfort and consolation.

They would know the Father (vv. 7-11)

The disciples had known Jesus, but they had not yet fully understood and appreciated his true significance. His soon-coming departure by means of the cross would secure for them — among other things! — a deeper and much more intimate knowledge of God. Knowledge of God comes, of course, through knowledge of Jesus because God and Jesus are one.

Philip may very well have taken Jesus' words about seeing the Father to indicate a visible display of God's glory. He may also have been connecting such a display with the establishment of an earthly kingdom. Jesus responded by telling Philip and the other disciples that they had seen in him something far greater than a visible emblem of God's glory because he, Jesus, was nothing less than God in flesh.

'The true knowledge of the Father cannot be obtained but by the true knowledge of the Son; and if the Son be really known, the Father is known also. The Father is known just so far as the Son is known — no farther'
(John Brown, *Discourses and Sayings of our Lord,*
vol. iii, pp.53-4).

They would do great works (v. 12)

This verse contains two assurances. Firstly, the disciples would continue the works of the Lord. Jesus said, 'Most assuredly, I say to you, he who believes in me, the works that I do he will do also...'

We have no difficulty understanding this. The disciples did indeed continue the miraculous works of Jesus. Simon Peter and John would heal a lame man (Acts 3:1-10); Peter would heal Aeneas (Acts 9:32-35) and raise Dorcas from the dead (Acts 9:36-43). The apostle Paul would perform many miracles (Acts 14:3; 16:16-18; 19:11-12).

It is the second part of the verse that causes us to be perplexed. Jesus also said: '...greater works than these he will do, because I go to my Father'. How could the disciples possibly do greater works than Jesus? We must look for the answer, not in the quality of the works, but rather in their quantity and scope. Our Lord's ministry was restricted to one tiny nation, Israel; but from those disciples it has fanned out to touch the whole world.

We must also keep in mind that the disciples' 'greater works' are still Jesus' works. They would be able to do these works because he was going to the Father. Every work of a believer is made possible by the glorified Christ.

'...Jesus was not thinking of better sermons or bigger miracles, but of something greater than both, something in which they would surpass what he accomplished in his earthly ministry. He was thinking, surely, of the *conversion* of men and women, both Jew and Gentile! Yes, the conversion of sinners to Christ is greater even than miracles of healing! Is conversion itself not a supernatural, sovereign work of God's grace? The unwilling are made willing in a day of God's power'

> (Gordon J. Keddie, vol. 2, p.107, italics are his).

Their prayers would be answered (vv. 13-14)

Some have taken this promise as a blank cheque to secure anything they want, but Jesus only obligates himself to answer prayers that are consistent with his name; that is, those that are prayed in keeping with his character and his will, and for his honour and glory. We must not expect, therefore, to have prayers answered that in any way compromise the name of Jesus or are contrary to what Scripture reveals to be his will.

'To apply to God for any thing in the name of Christ, the petition must be *in keeping with* what Christ is. We can only rightly ask God for that which will magnify His Son. To ask in the name of Christ is, therefore, to set aside our own will, and bow to the perfect will of God. If only we realized this more, what a *check* it would be on our ofttimes rash and ill-considered requests! How many of our prayers would never be offered did we but pause to inquire, Can I present *this* in *that* Name which is above every name?'

> (Arthur W. Pink, p.367, italics are his).

They would receive a helper (vv. 15-18)

Jesus had been their helper ('one called to be beside another'). His departure meant that the Holy Spirit would now come alongside them as their friend. He would come as 'the Spirit of truth', that is, with particular interest in and reference to the truths of God.

Jesus promised to send the Holy Spirit immediately after stressing the importance of keeping his commandments (v. 15). The disciples must have wondered how they could succeed in this. The Holy Spirit would indwell and enable them to do whatever Jesus would require.

> 'If we want the Holy Spirit to work in our lives, we must seek to glorify Christ; and we must make much of the Word of God … To be filled with the Spirit is the same as to be controlled by the Word. The Spirit of Truth uses the Word of truth to guide us into the will and the work of God'
>
> (Warren W. Wiersbe, vol. i, p.352).

DIGGING DEEPER

1. *Read verses 7-11. What is the relationship of Jesus and the Father?*

2. *Read verses 12-14. In what senses could the works of Jesus' disciples be greater than his own? What condition does Jesus attach to prayer?*

3. *Read verses 15-18. What information do these verses give us regarding the Holy Spirit?*

In the blanks provided, write 'T' for statements that are true and 'F' for those that are false.

_____ Thomas was the disciple who asked for a revelation of the Father (v. 8).

_____ Jesus spoke on his own authority (v. 10).

_____ Jesus promised that the disciples would do greater works than he had done (v. 12).

_____ If we love Jesus, we are to keep his commandments (v. 15).

_____ The world can receive the Holy Spirit (v. 17).

Five more reasons for comfort

'Peace I leave with you, my peace I give to you; not as the world gives do I give to you. Let not your heart be troubled, neither let it be afraid' (v. 27).

Jesus, knowing his disciples were crushed by the news that he was about to depart from this world, adds five additional reasons for them to be comforted. What a tender heart of concern he had for these men! He was touched and moved by their grief. As we examine the comfort he gave them, we can rest assured that he has that same tender concern for his disciples today.

They would see the Lord again (vv. 19-20)

Jesus' disciples may very well have found these words to be the most comforting: 'you will see me' (v. 19). They would only be separated from him for a while. They were destined to see him again and to live with him in the place of which he had spoken (v. 2). There they would have final and full knowledge of his relationship to God and their relationship to him (v. 20).

For this to take place, it was necessary for Jesus to live beyond the grave and for the disciples to do so as well. The resurrection of Jesus secured both. On one hand, it brought Jesus out of the grave, thereby enabling him to be seen. On the other hand, it guaranteed that the disciples would themselves live beyond the grave, thereby enabling them to do the seeing.

'The victory that Jesus won when He rolled the stone away and came forth from the tomb, was a victory not only for Himself but for His people. If the Head rose, much more shall the members'

(J. C. Ryle, vol. 3, p.85).

They would attain a higher level of communion (vv. 22-24)

Jesus' words about manifesting himself prompted Judas to ask: 'Lord, how is it that you will manifest yourself to us, and not to the world?' (v. 22).

William Hendriksen suggests that Judas was essentially saying this:

'Show thyself — thy great power — to the world. It may not be too late. Make an impression. Get into the limelight. Win applause. Overthrow the opposition'

(vol. ii, p.283).

Jesus responded to this question by emphatically declaring again the spiritual nature of his kingdom. It is established in the hearts of those who love him and keep his word. The singular pronouns in verses 23-24 show that the kingdom is set up in individuals. All who will receive it can have it!

Those who receive the kingdom are blessed with the presence of God (v. 23).

'There is more of heaven on earth to be obtained than most
Christians are aware of'

(J. C. Ryle, vol. 3, p.91).

The Holy Spirit would be their teacher (vv. 25-26)

Here Jesus gives more details about the Holy Spirit as
'the Spirit of truth' (v. 17). He, the Spirit, would give the
disciples understanding of the truth and would call to their
remembrance things that Jesus said. This, by the way, is
how we can be sure that the Gospels are accurate in their
portrayals of Jesus even though they were written many
years after he was crucified.

They were receiving his peace (v. 27)

Jesus, always a man of unruffled calm, was never 'stressed
out'. He now gives his disciples the peace that he himself
possessed. This was peace 'not as the world gives'.

The world can only wish us peace. It cannot actually
grant it. In those days, it was common for people to greet
each other by saying, 'Peace to you.' But that greeting could
not actually secure peace for those who heard it. One could
meet a thousand well-wishers in a day and still be anxious
and troubled.

With these words, Jesus actually bestowed peace on his
disciples. All we have to do to see the genuineness of his gift
is look at the accounts of these same men in the book of Acts.
There we find the peace of Jesus shining from them as they
time and again stand untroubled and unperturbed in the
midst of difficult circumstances.

We must not take Jesus' gift of peace to these men to mean that they had no responsibility in the matter. They could and would possess it as they exercised discipline over their hearts. That is the reason Jesus said, 'Let not your heart be troubled, neither let it be afraid.'

'The world's gifts concern only the body and time; Christ's gifts enrich the soul for eternity: the world gives lying vanities, and that which will cheat us; Christ gives substantial blessings, which will never fail us: the world gives and takes; Christ gives a good part that shall *never be taken away*'
(Matthew Henry, vol. v, p.1119, italics are his).

The Lord Jesus was going to his Father
(vv. 28-31)

The disciples thought they were sorrowing because of their love for Jesus. He puts a different light on it. If they loved him to the degree that they ought, they would rejoice! The fact that he was going back to the Father meant that the purpose for which he came (redemption) would soon be fulfilled and his time of suffering and hardship would be over. It should be noted here that the work of redemption could not be stopped by Satan himself (v. 30). We may picture Satan launching a final all-out assault at this late hour to divert Jesus from the cross, but he would find nothing in Jesus with which he could work, nothing he could use to jeopardize the work of redemption. There was no unwillingness in Jesus for the devil to work with. There was no disposition or thought in Jesus for Satan to use. The devil would come to Jesus, as it were, with a match in his hand to burn up the work of redemption; but there was no dry tinder or kindling in Jesus to which Satan could set the match.

DIGGING DEEPER

1. *Read verses 19-21. What comforting truths do you find in these verses?*

2. *Read verses 22-24. What is the mark of love for Christ? What does Jesus promise to the one who loves him?*

3. *Read verses 25-26. What additional information do these verses give us about the work of the Holy Spirit?*

4. *Read verses 27-28. What did Jesus promise to give his disciples? In what sense is the Father greater than Jesus?*

5. *Read verses 29-31. What do these verses teach about Jesus' commitment to the cross?*

Jesus identified the Holy Spirit as 'the Spirit of truth' (v. 17) and 'the Helper' (v. 26). Using the following verses, write in the blank spaces some other names for the Holy Spirit.

Genesis 1:2   _____

Zechariah 12:10 _____

Romans 1:4   _____

Romans 8:2   _____

Romans 8:9   _____

Romans 8:15   _____

Hebrews 9:14   _____

1 Peter 4:14   _____

Fourth quarter

Abiding in Jesus

'By this my Father is glorified, that you bear much fruit; so you will be my disciples' (v. 8).

The verses of this lesson carry us further into Jesus' last hours with his disciples on the night before he was crucified. These words, like those of the previous chapter, were designed to bring comfort to the disciples who were sorrowing over Jesus' impending departure.

Abiding in Jesus as the vine (vv. 1-8)

Jesus' opening words ('I am the true vine') give us the seventh and last of the 'I am' sayings in this Gospel.

With this figure the Lord Jesus assured his disciples that he would be achieving his purposes through them. Although he had promised to give the Holy Spirit to them, he did not want them to assume that they would be without his presence entirely. Indeed, they would be as vitally joined to him as branches are to a vine.

The disciples would prove that they were in this vital union with Christ by abiding in him. The departure of Judas Iscariot (13:26-30), which was still fresh on their minds, may have prompted Jesus to speak to them about two types of branches: those that truly abide and bear fruit (vv. 2,5), and those that do not (vv. 2,6). What does it mean to abide in Christ? It means continuing to believe, confess, obey, serve, love and worship him.

Continuance is the mark of reality. Those who continue in the faith prove that they have the faith. Those who do not continue are not truly connected to Christ even though they may outwardly appear to be. These will finally be 'cast out' and 'burned' (v. 6).

Even true branches do not produce fruit to the degree that they should. There are degrees of abiding in Christ. It is possible to be genuinely connected to Christ the vine and yet have a 'blockage' that hinders fellowship with him. Those who abide to a lesser degree can expect to be 'pruned' by God, the vinedresser (v. 1). The teaching and preaching of God's Word and the trials and afflictions of life are some of the ways God carries out this pruning.

Jesus' imagery of the vine and the branches enables us to come to several important principles:

- The purpose of God for us is that we should bear fruit for him; that is, that we should live to bring glory to him.
- Our sinful condition makes it impossible for us to bear the fruit God desires.
- To secure fruit from our lives, God has planted Jesus as the only true vine.
- The most important business in life is to make sure we are vitally connected to Christ.
- If we are connected to Christ, we shall abide or continue in him, bear fruit and be pruned so we can bear 'more' (v. 2) and 'much' fruit (v. 8).
- If we are not vitally connected to Christ, we will finally be 'burned' (v. 6).

- One of the privileges enjoyed by those who abide in Christ is answered prayer (v. 7). Those who allow Jesus' words to abide in them to a high degree will desire what he desires and will pray accordingly.

'In themselves believers have no life, or strength, or spiritual power. All that they have of vital religion comes from Christ. They are what they are, and feel what they feel, and do what they do, because they draw out of Jesus a continual supply of grace, help, and ability. Joined to the Lord by faith, and united in mysterious union with Him by the Spirit, they stand, and walk, and continue, and run the Christian race. But every jot of good about them is drawn from their spiritual Head, Jesus Christ'

(J. C. Ryle, vol. 3, pp.105-6).

Abiding in the love of Jesus (vv. 9-17)

The incentive (vv. 9,12-13,15-16)

Jesus called his disciples to abide in his love on the basis of his love for them. How had he loved them? Firstly, he loved them as the Father loved him (v. 9).

We can never fully comprehend the Father's love for the Son, but we can say at the very least that it was love without measure, without change and without end. And this is the way he loved those disciples, and, yes, loves his people today.

Secondly, Jesus loved them enough to lay down his life for them (v. 13). This is not in the same category as any other person laying down his life for someone else. When someone dies in that way, he is speeding up what is inevitable. In other words, he is choosing to die sooner the death he would inevitably face. When Jesus came to die for his people, he was doing something he did not have to do. Furthermore, he died in a special way. He died three deaths at the same time — physically, spiritually and eternally. On the cross, he received an eternity's worth of separation from God the Father.

Thirdly, Jesus loved them enough to call them his friends (vv. 13-14). Friendships are usually formed by the mutual choice of equals. Friendship with Jesus is the result of his choice (v. 16) of those who are anything but his equal.

The means (vv. 9-10,14,17)

How were the disciples to go about this matter of abiding in the love of Jesus? He provides this answer: 'If you keep my commandments, you will abide in my love...' (v. 10).

Keeping the commandments of Christ does not earn his love, but it does show that we belong to him. And it keeps our fellowship with him unimpeded.

The result (v. 11)

Satan would have us believe that obedience to Christ deprives us of true joy. The truth is the opposite.

> 'Joy is the flower of right; it is always and only the fruit of obedience to Christ, and in its essence it is a consciousness of his approving love'
>
> (Charles R. Erdman, p.134).

DIGGING DEEPER

1. *Read verses 1-6. How does Jesus identify himself in these verses? Identify the two ways in which we can be related to him. What becomes of those who are not properly related to him?*

2. *Read verse 7. What promise does Jesus give here?*

3. *Read verse 8. What does the production of spiritual fruit prove?*

4. *Read verses 9-11. How do we abide in the love of Christ? What results from the word of Christ?*

5. *Read verses 12-17. What are the evidences of Jesus' love for his disciples?*

Read Galatians 5:16-26. Write 'S' beside each quality that is fruit of the Spirit and 'F' beside each that is a work of the flesh.

_____ love
_____ adultery
_____ uncleanness
_____ hatred

_____ joy

_____ gentleness

_____ murder

_____ longsuffering

_____ kindness

_____ faithfulness

_____ drunkenness

_____ self-control

_____ goodness

_____ peace

_____ idolatry

_____ fornication

Hated for Jesus' sake

'If you were of the world, the world would love its own. Yet because you are not of the world, but I chose you out of the world, therefore the world hates you' (15:19).

The blessings offered by Christianity are incomparably glorious: forgiveness of sins, right standing with God, adoption into his family, access to God, the presence of the Holy Spirit, eternal life in heaven.

Yet Christianity also creates some serious difficulties. One of those is the hatred of the world for Christ and those who belong to him. The term 'world' refers to the society of those who form their values and engage in their pursuits without regard to God.

This disturbing reality is often swept under the carpet. Many preachers and teachers seek to attract people to the church by removing from the Christian message anything that makes them uncomfortable. The Lord Jesus, on the other hand, invariably put the cost of following him in the forefront (Matt. 16:24). In his concern to comfort his grieving disciples, Jesus never ignored reality. He refused to read the 'fine print' later.

Jesus would not downplay the world's hatred (note the number of times the word 'hate' appears in these verses), but he gave the disciples reasons to be comforted in the midst of it.

The certainty of this hatred (15:18)

By using the phrase 'If the world hates you,' Jesus was not suggesting any uncertainty. The word 'if' essentially means 'when'. Jesus made this abundantly clear when he said 'the world hates you' (15:19). He also said, 'If they persecuted me, they will also persecute you' (15:20).

The teaching of Jesus on this matter is echoed by the apostle Paul (Phil. 1:29; 2 Tim. 3:12).

> 'The favourites and heirs of heaven have never been the darlings of this world, since the old enmity was put between the seed of the woman and of the serpent'
>
> (Matthew Henry, vol. v, p.1129).

The reasons for this hatred (15:18-20)

The disciples were not of this world (15:19)

The world likes those who like it, that is, those who like the way it thinks and the way it acts. But it has very little tolerance for those who are out of step, those who think and act differently. And Christians do! They are not like the world because they have been chosen out of it to be the servants of the Lord Jesus Christ (15:19-20).

> 'The world system functions on the basis of conformity. As long as a person follows the fads and fashions and accepts the values of the world, he or she will "get along". But the Christian refuses to be "conformed to this world" (Rom. 12:2). The believer is a "new creation" (2 Cor. 5:17) and no longer wants to live the "old life" (1 Peter 4:1-4). We are the light of the world and the salt of the earth (Matt. 5:13-16), but

a dark world does not want light and a decaying world does not want salt! In other words, the believer is not just "out of step"; he is out of place!'

(Warren W. Wiersbe, vol. i, p.360).

The world hated the Lord Jesus (15:18)

The very fact that Jesus would be crucified the very next day is all the proof we need that the world hated him. The world that hates Jesus has to hate what belongs to him. Why did the world hate Jesus?

1. It was blinded to his true identity. It did not realize that he was sent by God (15:21; 16:3).

2. It could not tolerate his words (15:22). The Lord Jesus spoke about the reality of human sin, the certainty of divine judgement, the finality of his atoning death — truths the world finds distasteful and disturbing.

The enormity of this hatred (15:22-25)

It ignored convincing and powerful evidence (15:22,24)

Jesus was not saying that his haters would have been sinless if he had not come. He came because people were already sinners and needed a Saviour. He was rather saying that their existing sinfulness was greatly aggravated and intensified by his coming. The more light we have, the greater is the sin of rejecting it. The more truth we have, the fewer excuses we have for ignoring it. The people of Jesus' time were so flooded with evidence for the truth that they had to deliberately suppress it.

It was ultimately directed against God himself (15:23)

The very ones who were so emphatic in rejecting Jesus would have also been the most insistent that they were truly serving God in doing so. But here we have from the Lord Jesus himself the plain truth that hatred of him constitutes hatred of God. There is no division between Jesus and the Father. What does this tell us about those who maintain that it is possible to love God while rejecting Jesus?

The consolations in the midst of the hatred

The disciples would find the hatred of the world to be a reality, but, thank God, it would not be the only reality. They would also know the ministry of the Holy Spirit (15:26-27), who would both proceed from the Father and testify of the Son (there's that oneness again!). In the midst of persecution, the Holy Spirit would be there to assure the disciples that in standing for Jesus they would be standing for truth.

In addition to this, the disciples would also have the consolation of knowing that their persecution would itself prove the truth of their message (15:25), and it would demonstrate their faithfulness to their calling (15:27).

The depth of this hatred (15:20; 16:1-4)

Jesus did not want his disciples to 'stumble' (16:1). To be forewarned is to be forearmed. If Jesus had not foretold the hatred of the world, the disciples' faith could very well have been shaken when it appeared.

So Jesus minced no words. He told them that they were facing persecution (15:20), excommunication (16:2) and even martyrdom (16:2). The hatred would be so fierce that those who killed Christians would think, as we have noted, that they were serving God (16:2).

DIGGING   DEEPER

1. *Read 15:18-21. Why does the world hate the people of God?*

2. *Read 15:22. What do you understand this verse to be saying?*

3. *Read 15:23-24. What do these verses teach us about the relationship of Jesus to the Father?*

4. *Read 15:27. What consolations do believers have as they face the hatred of the world?*

5. *Read 16:1-2. What forms of persecution does Jesus identify?*

6. *Read 16:3-4. What truths can you glean from these verses?*

Find in the Scriptures indicated words to complete the following quote from J. C. Ryle:

'No Christian is in a healthy state of _____ [Phil.2:5] who is not prepared for _____ [1 Cor. 7:28] and _____ [2 Tim. 3:12]. He that expects to cross the troubled _____ [Song of Sol. 8:7] of this world, and to reach _____ [Col. 1:5] with wind and tide always in his favour, knows _____ [Phil. 4:6] yet as he ought to know. We never can tell what is before us in life. But of one thing we may be very sure; we must carry the _____ [Matt. 16:24] if we would wear the _____ [2 Tim. 4:8]'

(J. C. Ryle, vol. 3, p.148).

Additional teaching about the Holy Spirit

'Nevertheless I tell you the truth. It is to your advantage that I go away; for if I do not go away, the Helper will not come to you; but if I depart, I will send him to you' (v. 7).

Our salvation is the work of the triune God. The Father agreed to send the Son to this world; the Son agreed to come and provide salvation. The Holy Spirit agreed to come after the Son to apply and advance Jesus' finished work. In these verses, the Lord Jesus helps his disciples to understand both the necessity of the Holy Spirit's coming and the nature of his work.

The necessity of the Holy Spirit's coming (vv. 5-7)

Having affirmed again the hostility his disciples would face (vv. 1-4), Jesus returned to the subject of the Holy Spirit.

Jesus was disappointed with the disciples because of their slowness in spiritual things. They had not asked where he was going (v. 5). Did Jesus make a mistake? The disciples had indeed asked about his departure (13:36; 14:5). Jesus' point was that the disciples, because of their deep sorrow (v. 6), were more focused on the fact that he was departing than on the nature of the place to which he was going.

By doing so, they were only intensifying the sorrow and depriving themselves of blessing. As Jesus points out, his departure was necessary to further the plan of redemption (v. 7). This was cause for rejoicing.

The nature of the Holy Spirit's ministry (vv. 8-15)

Among unbelievers (vv. 8-11)

1. *Convincing of sin* (vv. 8-9). There can be no salvation until there is an awareness of sin. The whole plan of redemption assumes this and is predicated upon it. The word 'redemption' itself means 'to buy back'. It assumes that we have to be ransomed from something, and that something is sin.

> 'The doctrine and law of Christ cannot be received, except by those who are persuaded that they are sinners — guilty and depraved creatures — exposed to God's righteous displeasure — unfit for God's holy fellowship. The Gospel is throughout a restorative economy, and, therefore, can be understood, valued, accepted, only by those who are aware that the lost condition, for which such an economy is required and intended, is theirs'
>
> (John Brown, *Discourses*, vol. iii, p.416).

In connection with this part of the Spirit's work, the Lord specifically mentions the sin of not believing on him, that is, on Jesus (v. 9). Why did he mention this? Was he suggesting that God doesn't care about any other sins? The sin of rejecting Christ is essentially the embodiment or representation of all sin, and is the greatest of all.

John Brown says the Holy Spirit:

'...fixes the mind so on the meaning and evidence of the truth respecting Christ as to produce faith; and, in producing it, to lodge in the mind the conviction that, in not believing that truth, from the moment it was presented to it, there was sin, great sin; not merely intellectual mistake, but sin — deep, aggravated sin — the greatest sin man is capable of committing — indeed, a sin which, if persisted in, must end in hopeless perdition'

(*Discourses*, vol. iii, p.416).

2. *Convincing of righteousness* (v. 10). Those who crucified Jesus did so because they were persuaded that he was a wicked man who was deceiving others. Furthermore, they regarded themselves as being righteous in crucifying him. The fact that Jesus, after his resurrection, was received by the Father in heaven would serve as indisputable proof that their verdict on Jesus was wrong. The Holy Spirit would use the truth about Jesus to show his righteousness (v. 10).

'By means of *the resurrection* the Father would place the stamp of his approval upon his life and work (Acts 2:22,23,33; Rom. 1:4). He, the very One whom the world had branded as *unrighteous*, would by means of his victorious going to the Father be marked as *the Righteous One...*'

(William Hendriksen, p.326, italics are his).

3. *Convincing of judgement* (v. 11). The phrase 'ruler of this world' is a reference to Satan, who is also called 'the god of this age' (2 Cor. 4:4).

Satan ('adversary') is ever at work to convince people that Jesus is not the person he claims to be and the cross is of no significance. But that cross will prove to be the ruin of Satan. The Holy Spirit is presently showing sinners that Satan is a defeated foe, and all who share his rejection of Christ will share in his doom.

Among believers (vv. 12-15)

In addition to his ministry among unbelievers, the Holy Spirit would conduct a ministry among believers.

1. *Guiding into truth* (v. 13). The Holy Spirit would enable the disciples to declare accurately the truth about the Lord Jesus and his redeeming death on the cross. Some of the men who heard these words would write portions of the Bible (John, Matthew, Peter). How do we know that their writings are true? Jesus promised that the Holy Spirit would guide them! (see 2 Tim. 3:16; 2 Peter 1:20-21).

2. *Revealing the future* (v. 13). Those passages in which the human authors of Scripture were enabled to describe accurately the period stretching from Christ's first coming to his second must be considered a fulfilment of this promise (e.g. 2 Tim. 3:1-12; the book of Revelation).

3. *Glorifying Christ* (vv. 14-15). Some seem to have the idea that the Holy Spirit came into the world to 'do his own thing', that he is occupied with calling attention to himself. Nothing could be further from the truth. The Holy Spirit came to exalt Christ, and he is most pleased when we are Christ-centred and most grieved when we elevate anything or anyone above Christ — even if it is the Holy Spirit himself!

DIGGING DEEPER

1. *Read verses 5-6. What kept the disciples from inquiring more deeply into Jesus' departure?*

2. *Read verse 7. Why was the departure of Jesus advantageous for the disciples?*

3. *Read verses 8-11. On what points would the Holy Spirit bring conviction to unbelievers?*

4. *Read verses 12-15. What ministry would the Holy Spirit conduct among believers?*

Identify from each of the following verses a work of the Holy Spirit:

John 3:5-6   _____

Acts 9:31   _____

Romans 8:11   _____

Romans 8:16   _____

Romans 8:26   _____

Romans 8:26   _____

Ephesians 1:13 _____

Ephesians 1:14 _____

1 Corinthians 2:10 _____

1 Corinthians 12:3-11 _____

Jesus comforts his disciples

'Therefore you now have sorrow; but I will see you again and your heart will rejoice, and your joy no one will take from you' (v. 22).

With these verses we come to the end of the long discussion in which Jesus engaged with his disciples after washing their feet (13:1-30). The prevailing note in this discussion is comfort. The disciples were distraught and sorrowful as they contemplated the imminent departure of this one they so deeply loved.

The people of God today are as much in need of comfort as those men. While we are not in the same position as they were, we often feel that our circumstances are too much for us and we find it difficult to cope with them. However, in our struggles we can draw comfort from two things Jesus did for those men.

Jesus read their minds (vv. 16-19)

Jesus told his disciples that they would not see him for a little while and then they would see him again (v. 16). The 'little while' was, of course, the time from his death to his resurrection, after which he would appear to them again.

Although Jesus had mentioned his death and resurrection to the disciples on previous occasions, they still did not understand. Such is the slowness of the human heart when it comes to understanding spiritual things.

But the consoling thing for us at this point is that Jesus knew the thoughts racing through their minds before they ever expressed them. In the same way, the Lord also knows the pain of our hearts. He knows our circumstances, and he cares.

Jesus met their needs (vv. 20-33)

He gave them some promises (vv. 20-27)

1. *Their sorrow would be turned to unending joy* (vv. 20-22). Within a few hours the disciples would be taken over by a deep sense of grief. They would see their Lord snatched away from them and crucified. The very thing that would bring such deep sorrow to them would be a source of great joy to those who despised Jesus. It would not take long, however, for the tables to be turned. The Lord Jesus would rise from the dead on the third day, and the sorrow of the disciples would give way to inexpressible joy. That joy would be so great it would cause them to forget all about the sorrow they would feel immediately before it, even as a woman forgets the pain of childbirth when her baby finally arrives (v. 21).

Their sorrow would be temporary, but their joy would be permanent. No one would be able to take it from them. The resurrection of the Lord gives the believer permanent joy because it guarantees his final victory over everything that causes sorrow.

2. *They would have a new privilege in prayer* (vv. 23-24,26). To this point the disciples had brought their requests directly to Jesus, but the terms of their relationship with the Father would now be changed. By his resurrection ('in that day'), Jesus would make it possible for believers to address the Father on the basis of his finished work. They would no longer be as little children who needed Jesus to pray for them, but they would enjoy direct access to the Father themselves.

After the resurrection, the disciples were to pray in Jesus' name. This isn't a magical formula to tack on the end of prayer. When a believer closes his prayer in Jesus' name, he is essentially saying, 'I ask this on the basis of Christ's merits and in harmony with his redemptive work.'

We can be sure that those things that are truly in harmony with the nature of Christ and with his redemptive purpose will indeed be given by the Father.

'Of all the list of Christian duties there is none to which there is such abounding encouragement as prayer. It is a duty which concerns all. High and low, rich and poor, learned and unlearned — all must pray. It is a duty for which all are accountable. All cannot read, or hear, or sing; but all who have the spirit of adoption can pray … Let prayer in the name of Jesus be a daily habit with us every morning and evening of our lives. Keeping up that habit, we shall find strength for duty, comfort in trouble, guidance in perplexity, hope in sickness, and support in death'

(J. C. Ryle, vol. 3, p.171).

3. *They would have greater understanding* (vv. 25-28). The disciples were so filled with the idea of the Messiah setting up an earthly kingdom that they would have to see the

crucifixion and the resurrection before they would be able to fully understand. Until these events had taken place, it was as if Jesus had been speaking to them in proverbs or riddles.

After the resurrection, however, the disciples would see how totally mistaken were their notions of messiahship, and they would then be in a position to understand the Father and his plan. The Gospels and the Epistles are abundant evidence of this truth. The disciples could not have written these things until after the resurrection of Christ and the coming of the Holy Spirit.

He gave them a rebuke (vv. 29-32)

At this point the disciples felt Jesus was speaking with such clarity that they had come even then to full faith. Jesus told them not to be too sure of themselves, that they had not yet 'arrived'. This was proven by the fact that they fled from him in a matter of just a few hours.

He gave them a final assurance of his triumph (v. 33)

To undiscerning eyes the crucifixion would make it appear that wickedness had triumphed over Jesus. But that crucifixion would prove to be the means of his triumph, enabling Jesus to say, 'I have overcome the world.' This gave them a solid and sound basis for lasting peace.

> 'Never seek peace in the world. Even the men of the world do not find it there — far less will you. Seek it in Christ: there you are sure to find it; and when the world troubles you, say to your heart, "Return to thy rest"'
>
> (Brown, vol. iii, p.491).

DIGGING   DEEPER

1. Read verses 16-19. What period constituted the 'little while' during which the disciples would not see Jesus? What period constituted the 'little while' during which they would see him?

2. Read verses 20-22. What would the disciples experience during each of these two periods?

3. Read verses 23-26. What does Jesus promise in these verses? How would this privilege differ from what the disciples had previously experienced?

4. Read verses 27-33. What promises can you identify from these verses?

Unscramble the following to arrive at a quote from John Calvin:

Ew vaeh het rteah fo dgo sa noso sa ew clepa

___ ____ ___ ____ __ ____ __ ___ __ ___ ____

freebo imh eth maen fo sih nso.

_____ __ ___ ____ __ ___ ___.

WEEK 44
John 17:1-26

The Lord's Prayer

'And this is eternal life, that they may know you, the only true God, and Jesus Christ whom you have sent' (v. 3).

The opening words of John 18 indicate that Jesus prayed the prayer of chapter 17 while he and the disciples were still in the upper room. If that is the case, all eleven of his disciples heard it. Jesus had given them many words of comfort and encouragement prior to this prayer, but they probably found it to be more comforting than anything else Jesus said.

What went through the disciples' minds as they heard these words? They would almost certainly have thought about the importance of prayer. If Jesus found it necessary to pray, how much more should his disciples! They must also have thought about the great love the Lord Jesus had for them. Such tender words could only spring from deep love. They must have also noted Jesus' total trust in and calm reliance on the Father. John Calvin writes of Jesus:

'He, therefore, holds out an example to teachers, not to employ themselves only in sowing the word, but by mingling their prayers with it, to implore the assistance of God, that his blessing may render their labour fruitful'
(John Calvin, *Calvin's Commentaries*, vol. xviii, p.163).

'The exposition of the Word of God and prayer belong together. It is in prayer, costly, sustained and prevailing, that the Word of God is released through teaching and preaching. Prayer is the price of power, and the church of Jesus Christ is not likely to recover its lost authority until this basic biblical truth is recovered'

(Bruce Milne, *The Message of John*, p.237).

These might be classified as general impressions that lodged in the minds of the disciples as they listened to this prayer. However, there was also blessing and comfort for them in the specific requests that Jesus made and in the solemn resolve he exhibited.

The specific requests of Jesus

For the Father to be glorified (vv. 1-5)

Many have pointed out that Jesus prayed for himself in these verses because he says, 'Glorify your Son' (v. 1). But notice the reason Jesus wanted to be glorified. It was so he could, in turn, glorify the Father (v. 1).

The word 'glorify' means 'to honour' or 'to dignify'. The driving concern of Jesus' life was, therefore, to give honour to his Father. This was, of course, in keeping with the greatest commandment of all (Matt. 22:36-38).

In order for the Father to be glorified, Jesus knew it was necessary for him to finish the work the Father had sent him to do — the work of the cross! By that work he would secure the gift of eternal life for all those who were 'given' to him by the Father. What a blessing it is to realize God not only gave Jesus to us, but also, before the foundation of the world, gave all believers to the Lord Jesus!

We should not take Jesus' prayer for the Father to be glorified in the completion of his mission to mean he was uncertain about whether he would be able to complete it. Even before the work was completed Jesus was able to speak of it as though it were finished (v. 4).

For the disciples to be blessed

1. *The eleven* (vv. 6-19). After praying for the Father to be glorified, Jesus turned his attention to the eleven disciples who were with him. He prayed that they be kept or protected (vv. 11,15), that they be united (v. 11), that they experience his joy (v. 13) and that they be sanctified or separated from the world (v. 17).

Jesus prayed that his disciples would be kept because they were going to be in a world in which they would be hated (v. 14), a world which was under the control of 'the evil one' (v. 15). He prayed that they be sanctified ('set apart') because this evil world also carries a strange attraction for believers and has the power to draw them away from faithfulness to Christ. If believers are to maintain purity in such a world, they must immerse themselves in the Word of God.

2. *Future disciples* (vv. 20-24). How comforting it is to realize Jesus included us in his prayer! In these verses, we can see two distinct petitions Jesus offered for his future disciples. Firstly, he prayed for their unity (v. 21). Some Christians tend to believe that Jesus was referring here to organizational unity, and that the only way we will ever attain this is if we get rid of all denominational distinctions and belong to one church. But surely we realize even this does not guarantee unity. It is possible to be members of one church and still be divided.

On the other hand, Christians who belong to different denominations do not necessarily find themselves divided.

There is a oneness and a kinship among all true Christians regardless of their denominational distinctions.

Why was Jesus concerned so much about unity? It is an indispensable ingredient for the effective preaching of the gospel.

'Discord and division become no Christian. For wolves to worry the lambs is no wonder, but for one lamb to worry another, this is unnatural and monstrous'

(Thomas Brooks,
cited by Warren W. Wiersbe, vol. i, p.371).

Jesus also prayed that his disciples would share his glory. This petition will finally be fulfilled when we get to heaven.

The solemn resolve of Jesus (vv. 25-26)

Jesus concluded his prayer by resolving to declare the Father's name. He had, of course, declared it to the disciples throughout his period of association with them, and he was determined to continue to declare it. By his death on the cross, his resurrection, his post-resurrection appearances, his ascension and his gift of the Holy Spirit to his church, the Lord Jesus abundantly kept this resolve.

DIGGING   DEEPER

1. Read verses 1-5. What is 'the hour' to which Jesus referred? What did Jesus want this hour to accomplish? In what ways did this hour accomplish what Jesus desired?

2. *Read verses 6-19. For whom does Jesus pray in these verses? How does he describe them? What does he ask for them?*

3. *Read verses 20-24. For whom does Jesus pray in these verses? What does he ask for them?*

4. *Read verses 25-26. What resolve does Jesus express?*

In the puzzle below, circle five of the key words from Jesus' prayer:

```
T  O  W  C  P  W  R  K  E  P  T
G  I  V  E  N  H  G  R  S  O  N
D  L  U  M  N  B  T  S  V  Z  F
I  Y  O  T  Q  B  D  T  I  R  A
Q  Q  K  R  U  I  S  G  H  N  T
U  Z  V  W  I  S  E  J  C  I  H
M  X  C  H  V  F  X  J  K  L  E
A  G  J  L  B  C  I  O  Y  T  R
O  W  R  A  N  N  Y  E  A  Z  C
P  L  K  X  E  U  I  F  D  R  M
```

Jesus betrayed and denied

'So Jesus said to Peter, "Put your sword into the sheath. Shall I not drink the cup which my Father has given me?"' (v. 11).

After Jesus prayed for his disciples in the upper room, he went with them to the Garden of Gethsemane where he engaged in fervent prayer to the Father as his disciples slept.

It was there in the garden that Jesus was seized and arrested by a delegation sent by 'the chief priests and Pharisees' and led by Judas Iscariot. From the garden, he was first taken to Annas, then to Caiaphas and finally to Pilate. Three major truths stand out in these events.

The sovereign majesty of Jesus (vv. 4-9,11)

His perfect knowledge (v. 4)

Jesus wasn't taken by surprise at the appearance of Judas and his detachment. He knew beforehand that they would be coming, and he knew exactly what lay ahead of him during the remaining hours of the night and throughout the next day. Knowing all this, he still 'went forward' (v. 4).

What a glorious picture this is! Our Saviour, knowing all the terrible suffering at hand, willingly stepped forward to perform the work of redemption. Such was his inexpressible love for sinners!

His glorious person (v. 6)

When the mob identified Jesus of Nazareth as the one whom they were seeking, Jesus responded: 'I am he.' The men of the mob then 'drew back and fell to the ground'.

Jesus was, of course, fully God and fully man. His deity was, as it were, clothed in humanity. On this occasion, a beam of divinity flashed through Jesus' humanity and flattened these men.

His caring heart (vv. 8-9)

Jesus stepped forward, identified himself and said of the disciples, 'Let these go their way.' We may picture him stepping between his arresters and his disciples. This provides a beautiful picture of his death on the cross. There he took our sins so we might freely go our way.

His complete submission (v. 11)

The 'cup' the Lord Jesus Christ was given to drink was the cross. It was given to him by the Father, and even though it contained anguish and agony we will never know, Jesus submitted to it.

'This "cup" is the cup of the wine of God's wrath (Ps. 75:8; Is. 51:17; Jer. 25:15-17,27-38). The "cup" that Jesus chooses to drink is not merely death, but the wrath of God upon sin...'
                                        (*The Geneva Study Bible*, p.1699).

The sad blindness of unbelievers
(vv. 3,19-24)

These verses present us with several who had never truly accepted Jesus. There was poor, pathetic Judas. He had seen Jesus perform miracle after miracle and had walked with him for three and a half years, but he had never come to a true and living faith.

> 'When people today pretend to know and love the Lord, they are committing the sin of Judas. It is bad enough to betray Christ, but to do it with a kiss, a sign of affection, is the basest treachery of all. It was born in the pit of hell'
>   (Warren W. Wiersbe, vol. i, p.373).

Those in the delegation sent to arrest Jesus experienced the glory of Jesus in the process but still refused to acknowledge his Lordship.

Then there was Annas, whom John calls the high priest. This seems to be in conflict with other verses in which John refers to Caiaphas as the high priest (11:49; 18:24). In all likelihood this was John's way of saying that even though Caiaphas was technically the high priest, he was under the control of Annas, who was his father-in-law.

Annas also shows us the tragic blindness of the unbeliever. He questioned Jesus about his teaching as if there were some great mystery about it, but, as Jesus pointed out, his teaching had been open and clear.

Each of these — Judas, the mob and Annas — had more than sufficient evidence for turning from their course of opposition to Jesus. But each turned a deaf ear toward the evidence and drove madly ahead.

The tragic frailty of the saints
(vv. 10,15-18,25-27)

The arrival of the mob and the subsequent arrest of Jesus plunged Simon Peter into a period of sad failure. Firstly, he drew his sword, lunged forward, swung wildly, and, with numerous authorities within easy range, succeeded only in whacking off the ear of a poor servant (v. 10). This poor man was probably the only one in the whole group who did not want to be there!

Jesus rebuked Peter and healed the ear; but this was not Simon Peter's only failing that night, as he proceeded to deny three times his connection with Jesus (vv. 15-18,25-27).

'It is easy to point the finger of scorn at the great apostle; but there are few of the followers of Christ who in times of less severe testing have not as truly denied their Lord by word and deed, with cowardice, and deceit and passion'
(Charles R. Erdman, *The Gospel of Matthew*, p.214).

In cutting off the servant's ear, Simon Peter was guilty of doing something Jesus *had not* commanded. Seeing the mob fall back from Jesus should have been enough to convince Peter that Jesus did not need his protection. Had Jesus wanted to escape, one word from his mouth would have been more potent than all the disciples swinging swords.

In denying Jesus, Peter was guilty of failing to do something Jesus *had* commanded. Jesus had made it clear that his church was to be built upon the confession that he is the Son of God (Matt. 16:13-18). Peter had the opportunity to confess but did not do so.

Many churches today seem to have fallen into these same errors. They commit the first by seeking to advance the kingdom through means Christ has not commanded and the second by failing to confess the true gospel.

DIGGING   DEEPER

1. *Read verses 1-3. Where did Judas find Jesus? Who was with Judas? Who was with Jesus?*

2. *Read verses 4-6. What happened when Jesus identified himself?*

3. *Read verses 7-9. What significance does John attach to the disciples being allowed to 'go their way'?*

4. *Read verses 10-11. Why was Simon Peter mistaken to use his sword?*

5. *Read verses 12-14,19-24. How were Annas and Caiaphas related? How did Jesus respond to Annas' inquiry about his teaching?*

6. *Read verses 15-18,25-27. Where did Simon Peter first deny Jesus? Where did the second and third denials take place? What is the significance of the rooster crowing?*

Across:

3. What happened after Simon's third denial

5. Simon Peter's weapon

Down:

1. The words Jesus used to identify himself

2. The high priest's servant

4. The high priest that year

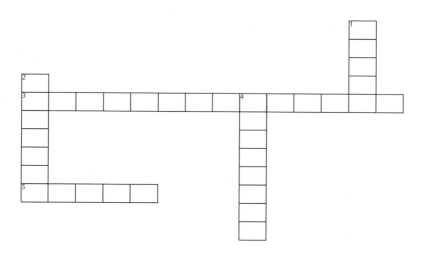

Jesus unjustly condemned

'Pilate therefore said to him, "Are you a king then?" Jesus answered, "You say rightly that I am a king. For this cause I was born, and for this cause I have come into the world, that I should bear witness to the truth. Everyone who is of the truth hears my voice"' (18:37).

Jesus is here before Pilate, the Roman governor of the Jewish state. The Sanhedrin had already condemned Jesus to death but they desperately wanted Pilate's approval. On occasions the Jews would execute someone without Rome's approval (Acts 7:54-60). Why, then, did they desire Rome's approval before executing Jesus? They may have feared his popularity would create a backlash against them if they did it on their own.

However, the more likely answer is that they wanted Jesus to be executed in the official Roman way — crucifixion. Crucifixion was designated in Scripture as a sign of God's curse (Deut. 21:23). If Jesus were crucified it would effectively end all talk of him being the Messiah. To them a crucified Messiah was as impossible as a square circle.

By the wickedness of the religious leaders

John does not explicitly mention the charge the Jews were bringing against Jesus, but it is clear from Pilate's first question that it was treason. Jesus was supposedly setting himself up as a king in opposition to Caesar.

This charge shows us the massive hypocrisy of the religious leaders. They hated the Romans, and someone opposing Caesar was the least of their concerns. The reason they wanted Jesus crucified had nothing to do with him seeking to establish a political kingdom, but rather with his claim to be the Son of God, which they regarded as blasphemous. Knowing that religious issues would mean nothing to Pilate, they re-fashioned the charge in terms he could not ignore, namely, that Jesus was a political revolutionary who was guilty of inciting rebellion against Rome.

In response to the question of whether he was a king, Jesus responded by essentially saying, 'Yes, but not the kind you think' (v. 36).

Pilate and the Jews had one thing in common. When they thought about a king, they thought solely in terms of an earthly kingdom. Jesus made it clear that his kingdom was not of this earth. It was and is a spiritual kingdom that is built on the truth of God.

By the weakness of Pilate

'Let justice be done though the heavens fall!' was a Roman motto. But it is obvious Pilate was more concerned with protecting himself and his job than he was with justice.

Pilate's initial conversation with Jesus convinced him that Jesus was innocent of the charges brought against him. From that moment he set about to release him.

He first resorted to the Passover custom of releasing a prisoner (18:39-40), asking the people to decide between Jesus and Barabbas. The latter was probably chosen because he had a particularly unsavoury reputation.

With that ploy having failed, Pilate decided to scourge Jesus and then bring him before the people (19:1-6). The scourge consisted of a leather whip with pieces of metal and bone. It was so terrible that many prisoners died in the process.

Few sights were more pathetic than that of a scourged man, but the hearts of the Jews were so hard that they were not moved even by this sickening sight.

> 'What man could behold a scourged prisoner and still want the victim crucified? Pilate probably thought the answer to that was "No one" ... "Behold the man!" carries the idea, "Look at this poor fellow! Hasn't he suffered enough? Take pity on Him and let me release Him"'
>
> (Warren W. Wiersbe, vol. i, pp.379-80).

Pilate had the authority to release Jesus. All he needed was the moral courage to do the right thing, but he could not bring himself to do this. When the Jews raised the possibility of him being disloyal to Caesar (19:12), Pilate showed his true colours. All concerns for justice evaporated as he caved in to the pressure. He washed his hands of the crime, but that water could not remove the cowardice of his heart.

By the will of God

In the face of Pilate's repeated attempts to release Jesus, the Jews finally blurted out the real reason they wanted him crucified: 'He made himself the Son of God' (19:7). This statement caused Pilate great consternation.

> 'The Romans and Greeks had numerous myths about gods coming to earth as men (note Acts 14:8-13), so it is likely

that Pilate responded to the phrase "Son of God" with these stories in mind. Already the governor had been impressed by the words and demeanor of our Lord; he had never met a prisoner like him before. Was he indeed a god come to earth? Did he have supernatural powers?'

(Warren W. Wiersbe, vol. i, p.380).

These fearful thoughts drove Pilate to attempt to intimidate Jesus: 'Do you not know that I have power to crucify you, and power to release you?' (19:10). To this stormy assertion our Lord calmly responded that Pilate had no power to do anything other than that which God had already determined should be done. The crucifixion was, therefore, at one and the same time the work of wicked men and the plan of God (Acts 2:23).

DIGGING DEEPER

1. *Read 18:28-32. Why did the Jewish leaders bring Jesus to Pilate? How did this work towards the fulfilment of prophecy?*

2. *Read 18:33-38. What did Jesus say about his kingdom? What do you think Pilate meant when he said, 'What is truth?'*

3. *Read 18:39 - 19:7. What was Pilate seeking to accomplish in these verses? Why did the Jews want Jesus crucified?*

4. *Read 19:8-11. What was Pilate attempting to do here? How did Jesus respond?*

5. *Read 19:12-16. What argument did the Jews use to force Pilate to crucify Jesus?*

Locate the following verses and write in the blanks provided the examples of what various people were told to 'behold':

John 1:29   _____

John 12:15   _____

Luke 24:39   _____

The crucifixion of Jesus

'Now Pilate wrote a title and put it on the cross.
And the writing was:
JESUS OF NAZARETH,
THE KING OF THE JEWS' (19:19).

The apostle John was an eyewitness of the crucifixion of Jesus. It seems likely that he was the only one of the Gospel writers who was there. The details he shares in these verses make it clear that he was present.

General details (vv. 17-24)

Crucifixion was an indescribably horrible means of execution, so much so that no Roman citizen was permitted to suffer it even if he committed the most heinous of crimes. But John conveys very few of the horrors of Jesus' crucifixion, mentioning only the following four points.

The place (v. 17)

The hill of Golgotha, located outside Jerusalem, was called 'the Place of a Skull' because its indentations gave it the appearance of a skull.

The placement (v. 18)

The position of Jesus' cross in relation to those of the two crucified with him was no coincidence. The fact that Jesus' cross was in the centre of those of the two thieves, one of whom accepted him and one of whom rejected him, depicts Jesus as the divider of men.

The inscription that Pilate wrote (vv. 19-22)

This became a matter of controversy. To the Jewish leaders, it appeared to take Jesus' claims at face value. They wanted the inscription to indicate only that he claimed to be king. These men represent all those who object to any claim of absolute truth. Such people want Christians to say of Christianity: 'This is our opinion' and not 'This is truth.'

The soldiers dividing Jesus' garments (vv. 23-24)

These men may be taken as representatives of all those who are so occupied with mere trivialities that they are oblivious to spiritual and eternal realities. While Jesus was making it possible for sinners to wear the garment of righteousness, they were satisfied to seek a garment that would provide covering for them for only a brief time in this world.

> 'Poor, poor soldiers! How much did they take home from Calvary? A few pieces of clothing! No truly penitent hearts, no renewed visions, no changed lives, no Savior? Even today, how much — or how little — do some people carry home with them from the church service, the Bible class, the hymn sing, the revival meeting'
>
> (William Hendriksen, *Luke*, p.1029).

Little did these men realize that their interest in the garments of Jesus gave yet another indication that he was indeed the Son of God, fulfilling the prophecy of Psalm 22:18. The fulfilment of prophecy is one of the major proofs for the claims of Jesus. It has been calculated that Jesus fulfilled twenty major prophecies of the Old Testament in the twenty-four-hour period that ended in his death, and approximately 325 prophecies in his life and ministry.

A special word (vv. 25-27)

'Now there stood by the cross of Jesus his mother...' (v. 25). Are there any words more heart-wrenching than these? Jesus was dying the most horrid, ignominious death possible and his mother was there to see it.

We are blessed when the trials of life swell up around us if we have faithful friends on whom we can depend to the very end, as Mary had. Her sister was there, as were Mary Magdalene and John, who consistently identifies himself as 'the disciple whom Jesus loved'.

Suddenly Jesus looked upon that little company and spoke to his mother: 'Woman, behold your son!' He must have nodded towards John as he spoke those words. And then, nodding towards Mary, he said to John: 'Behold your mother!'

These few words first show the tender concern of the Lord Jesus for those who have pressing, urgent needs. Mary had such needs. The future must have looked very bleak to her as she stood there watching her son die. Her husband had died. Her other sons had not yet accepted Jesus as the Messiah, and she may well have been unable to count on them for either physical or emotional support. And now Jesus was being taken from her.

What was to become of her? Jesus provided the answer by placing Mary in John's care and by charging John to treat her as though she were his own mother. His words found their mark for the next thing we read is, 'from that hour that disciple took her to his own home'.

These words also reveal the priority Jesus gives to preparing for the next life. This lesson comes out in a couple of ways. Firstly, the fact that Jesus was concerned about Mary and her physical needs did not cause him to come down from the cross and abandon the work of redemption he was performing there.

The second indication that Jesus gave priority to the next life arises from the way in which he addressed Mary. He does not address her as 'mother' but simply as 'woman'. His purpose in doing so may very well have been to reflect the new order of things. From this point forward, Mary was in a sense no longer his mother but only a believer.

'He provided for her as a Saviour a million times better home than He provided for her as a son'
(Herschel W. Ford, *Seven Simple Sermons on the Saviour's Last Words*, pp.38-9).

DIGGING DEEPER

1. *Read verses 17-18. Where was Jesus crucified? How many were crucified with him?*

2. *Read verses 19-22. Why did the Jews object to Pilate's inscription? How did he respond?*

3. *Read verses 23-24. What is the significance of the soldiers gambling for Jesus' garments?*

4. *Read verses 25-27. What did Jesus do in these verses?*

Write beside the Scripture references the other words Jesus spoke while he was on the cross.

Matthew 27:46 _____

Luke 23:34 _____

Luke 23:43 _____

John 19:28 _____

John 19:30 _____

Luke 23:46 _____

The death and burial of Jesus

'So when Jesus had received the sour wine, he said, "It is finished!" And bowing his head, he gave up his spirit' (19:30).

With these verses, John adds additional words from Jesus while he was on the cross and gives us details about the piercing of his side and his burial.

Additional words from Jesus (vv. 28-30)

'I thirst'

Jesus' thirst was real. It had been a period of several hours since he had last touched a cup to his lips — probably when he had supper with his disciples. His real thirst means his humanity was real, and true humanity was essential for him to provide atonement for sinners. He could not have done anything for us had he not been one of us.

This cry also fulfilled prophecy. We get the impression that Jesus was keeping a mental checklist. He had already suffered the wrath of God on behalf of sinners, but one more thing remained. The redemption that he was providing by his death had been anticipated in the Old Testament in striking detail. Included in those anticipations was the promise that he would be given vinegar to drink (Ps. 69:21). To this point there had not been any offer of vinegar. In order to prompt this fulfilment, Jesus cried, 'I thirst!' The cry had its desired effect. The vinegar was immediately offered, and Jesus drank of it. It is no accident that John writes: 'So when Jesus had received the sour wine, he said, "It is finished!"' (John 19:30).

We must not think of Jesus as only a passive victim while he was on the cross. He actively worked at his death to make sure it was exactly as the Father had promised it would be. It is tempting to think of Christ as a conductor and the various details of his crucifixion as instruments in an orchestra. Under his leadership, all the details are brought into harmony without so much as a single discordant note.

His minute fulfilment of so many prophecies compels us to confess that he is exactly what the Bible proclaims him to be — the eternal Son of God. If he is the Son of God, we are led inexorably to another conclusion — what he says is true and must be obeyed.

'It is finished'

It is not too much to say that from the moment the Father, the Son and the Holy Spirit agreed upon the plan of redemption they began to look forward to one word being spoken. That word, *'tetelestai'*, is translated with three words in English: 'It is finished.'

All the promises and types of the Old Testament looked forward to that word. Jesus left heaven and took our humanity for the sole purpose of uttering that word. All that he did during his earthly life and ministry was in preparation for that word. He endured the intense agony of Gethsemane and the anguish of the cross so that he could utter that one word.

Jesus has been on the cross for six long hours. Every prophecy has been fulfilled. The wrath of God has been endured in fullest measure. That cup is now empty. And Jesus cries: 'It is finished!' All of heaven has been focused on that cry, and it is now uttered. Heaven cheers. Hell trembles.

When the Lord Jesus Christ said, 'It is finished,' he was not speaking as a tortured man who was glad to see suffering come to an end. His death did not merely end something. It accomplished something, namely, the provision of redemption for sinners.

'And thus was finished the greatest and most wonderful thing that was ever done. Now the angels beheld the most wonderful sight that ever they saw. Now was accomplished the main thing that had been pointed at by the various institutions of the ceremonial law, by all the typical dispensations, and by all the sacrifices from the beginning of the world...

'Then was finished that great work, the purchase of our redemption, for which such great preparation had been made from the beginning of the world. Then was finished all that was required in order to satisfy the threatenings of the law, and all that was necessary in order to satisfy divine justice; then the utmost that vindictive justice demanded, even the whole debt, was paid. Then was finished the whole of the purchase of eternal life. And now there is no need of any thing more to be done towards a purchase of salvation for sinners; nor has ever any thing been done since, nor will any thing more be done for ever and ever'

(Jonathan Edwards, *The Works of Jonathan Edwards*,
The Banner of Truth Trust, vol. i, p.580).

The piercing of Jesus' side (vv. 31-37)

It was the custom of the Romans to leave those crucified to decay and be devoured by the birds. But the law of Moses required that anyone hanged on a tree should not be left there (Deut. 21:22-23). While the Jewish leaders had no scruples about breaking the law when it served their ends, they were very scrupulous about keeping it at other points. On this point they were scrupulous. They went to Pilate and asked that the legs of Jesus and those crucified with him be broken. This would prevent them from being able to push up with their legs, thus relieving the pressure on their diaphragms. Death would then come very quickly from suffocation.

When the soldiers came to break the legs of Jesus, it was apparent that he was already dead. We can imagine the conversation. One soldier says, 'There is no need to break his legs. He's dead.' A second says: 'How can you be sure?' The first, with spear in hand, says, 'I'll make sure,' and thrusts the spear into Jesus' side.

This piercing fulfilled prophecy in two ways: his bones were not broken (Ps. 34:20; Exod. 12:46; Num. 9:12) and his side was pierced (Zech. 12:10).

The fact that blood and water poured from his side (v. 34) was significant. Blood represents atonement and water represents purification. By his death Jesus made atonement for sinners and purifies them from their sins.

The burial of Jesus (vv. 38-42)

We are specifically told that Joseph of Arimathea was a secret disciple for fear of the Jews. The same was probably true of Nicodemus. But they both openly showed their allegiance. They must have realized that the public humiliation of Jesus could not be repaid with silent, secret discipleship. Have we studied Calvary's love long enough to come away from half-hearted, careful discipleship?

Verse 41 takes us full circle. The plan of redemption was announced in a garden at a time when life had turned into death (Gen. 3). Here it comes to fulfilment in a garden where death is about to turn into life.

DIGGING DEEPER

1. *Read verses 28-30. What is the significance of these two cries from Jesus?*

2. *Read verses 31-34. Why did the Jewish leaders want Jesus' legs broken? Why did the Romans not break his legs?*

3. *Read verses 35-37. How does the apostle John identify himself? What significance did he find in Jesus' legs not being broken?*

4. *Read verses 38-40. How do you explain the boldness of Joseph and Nicodemus in the burial of Jesus?*

5. *Read verses 41-42. Where was the tomb of Jesus? Why was there an element of hurry in his burial?*

Draw a line to connect the following aspects of Jesus' crucifixion as reported by John with the Old Testament verses in which they were prophesied:

The dividing of his garments   Zechariah 12:10

Thirst   Isaiah 53:9

His legs not broken   Psalm 22:18

His side pierced   Psalm 69:21

His burial with the rich   Psalm 34:20

Evidences for the resurrection of Jesus

'Then the other disciple, who came to the tomb first, went in also; and he saw and believed' (v. 8).

Christianity rises or falls on the resurrection of Jesus. This does not mean that our faith is in jeopardy. The resurrection is based on the most solid evidence imaginable. In this passage, John puts before us some of that evidence.

Evidence related to the tomb (vv. 1-10)

The stone was rolled away (vv. 1-2)

When Mary Magdalene went to the tomb early in the morning of the first day of the week, she was not prepared for what she found. The heavy stone covering the opening of the tomb had been rolled away. We can be sure that the stone was not removed to let Jesus out, but rather to let the disciples in!

Although Jesus had promised his resurrection, Mary Magdalene interpreted the removal of the stone to mean someone had removed his body (v. 2). And she ran to Simon Peter to report as much.

The evidence inside the tomb (vv. 3-10)

Upon hearing Mary's words, Simon Peter and John ran to the tomb. John arrived first but paused at the opening to look inside. The impetuous Simon Peter brushed past him and 'went into the tomb' (v. 6). What he did *not* see, coupled with what he *did* see, were utterly convincing. What he did *not* see was Jesus' body. What he *did* see was a convincing configuration of the linen strips in which Jesus' body had been wrapped, and which evidently retained the shape of the body without it being there. And the cloth which had been used to cover his face was neatly folded and set aside.

When John entered the tomb, he needed only one glance at those wrappings to be convinced that Jesus had risen (v. 8). John adds, probably to his considerable embarrassment, that he and Simon Peter had not believed in the resurrection until that moment (v. 9).

We must not miss the significance of John returning to his home. To understand this we only have to recall the words of John 19:25-27.

'At the home of John there is someone who must have been overjoyed to hear the story. That "someone" was ... Mary, the mother of Jesus'

(William Hendriksen, vol. ii, p.451).

A resurrection appearance (vv. 14-18)

The sorrow of Mary (vv. 14-15)

By the time Mary Magdalene returned to the tomb, Simon Peter and John had already departed. She evidently did not encounter them on her way back to the tomb because she obviously arrived at the tomb clinging to her mistaken theory (v. 13). So deep was her grief that she stood weeping outside the tomb of Jesus.

Mary, out of whom Jesus had cast seven demons (Mark 16:9), should have known Jesus had the power to conquer death as he had promised. But she failed to consider either his power or his promises. His death was to her final and irreversible, and there was nothing to do but sob.

The tragedy of Mary's unbelief was compounded by the fact that she looked into the tomb and saw two angels and no body (vv. 11-12). This was powerful evidence, but Mary seems to have been looking hard for reasons not to believe.

She persisted in her unbelief when the Lord Jesus himself appeared to her. Supposing him to be the gardener, she asked him to show her where he had hidden the body (vv. 14-15).

The grace of Jesus (v. 16)

The Lord Jesus wiped away Mary's sorrow simply by calling her name. Her unbelief made her deserving of a stern rebuke, but the Lord Jesus did not reprimand her. His presence was rebuke enough! How foolish Mary must have felt! Death had not won. It was not final and irreversible. The Lord Jesus had defeated it just as he promised. Here is solace for everyone who has lost a believing loved one. The resurrection of Jesus guarantees that all who know him will be resurrected to eternal glory (John 14:19).

The response of Mary (vv. 17-18)

Mary at first responded to the Lord by apparently wrapping her arms around him as if she would never let him go. A gentle rebuke from Jesus was sufficient for her to release him.

325

William Hendriksen explains the rebuke of Jesus in this way:

> 'What he condemned was Mary's mistaken notion that the former mode of fellowship was going to be resumed, in other words, that Jesus would once again live in daily visible association with his disciples, both men and women. The fellowship, to be sure, would be resumed; but it would be far richer and more blessed. It would be the communion of the ascended Lord in the Spirit with his Church'
>
> (vol. ii, p.455).

After Jesus spoke to her, Mary went to tell his disciples. Let us learn from this that we do not respond properly to the truth of Christianity simply by basking in it, but rather by trumpeting it all around.

DIGGING DEEPER

1. *Read verses 1-2. What did Mary Magdalene find at the tomb of Jesus? What did she do?*

2. *Read verses 3-9. What did Peter and John do when they heard Mary's report? What did John and Peter see in the tomb?*

3. *Read verse 10. What did John and Peter do after they saw the tomb?*

4. *Read verses 11-13. What did Mary do when she returned to the tomb? What evidence did she ignore?*

5. *Read verses 14-16. What finally convinced Mary that Jesus had risen?*

6. *Read verses 17-18. Why did Jesus tell Mary to stop clinging to him? What did Mary do after Jesus spoke to her?*

Circle in the puzzle below four key terms in John 20:1-18:

B	U	P	R	Z	D	E	F	G	H	I	K	L
T	L	I	N	E	N	C	L	O	T	H	S	A
O	V	A	S	A	N	T	Q	C	P	G	R	I
M	V	X	Z	I	Y	P	M	K	H	J	T	I
B	A	T	Y	U	M	A	S	Q	U	T	R	V
Q	P	I	N	B	V	O	D	R	Z	X	M	V
U	I	H	J	K	B	C	N	I	Y	P	K	L
M	A	R	Y	M	A	G	D	A	L	E	N	E

Appearances of the living Saviour

'Jesus said to him, "Thomas, because you have seen me, you have believed. Blessed are those who have not seen and yet have believed"' (v. 29).

These verses relate two meetings which the risen Lord had with his disciples, the second of which moved Thomas from doubt to faith. Thomas' experience then gave the apostle John the perfect basis for stating the purpose behind his Gospel.

Jesus' first meeting with his disciples (vv. 19-23)

To give them evidence for his resurrection (vv. 19-20)

The fear of these men is not surprising. They knew that the same authorities which had torn Jesus from them and crucified him would not hesitate to eliminate them as well.

They did not remain long in the clutches of fear. Jesus suddenly appeared without making use of the door (which they would probably have refused to answer). He immediately said, 'Peace be with you,' (v. 19) and showed them his hands and side (v. 20).

There was something about the hands and feet of Jesus which made it immediately apparent that he had risen. The wounds he had received when he was crucified were still visible! Those wounds indicate something of the greatness of Jesus' redeeming work. When he took our humanity, he took it for ever! He is still in that humanity. If we could see him now, we would see those same pierced hands and feet.

What a marvel Jesus' resurrected body was! He could pass through closed doors with a body that still bore the marks of the crucifixion! Jesus' word of peace and the sight of his hands and feet generated in the minds of the fearful disciples the following deduction, or syllogism:

Major premise: If Jesus is here, he must have risen.
Minor premise: If Jesus has risen, he must be Lord of all.
Conclusion: If Jesus is Lord of all, there is no need to fear anything or anyone.

To give them assurance for the future (vv. 21-23)

Jesus was not content merely to allay his disciples' fear. He also assured them that they would soon be ministering to the very men of whom they had been so afraid. The knowledge of his resurrection and the gift of the Holy Spirit were all they would need to become faithful witnesses.

If Jesus gave his disciples the Holy Spirit on this occasion, how are we to explain the coming of the Holy Spirit on the Day of Pentecost? (Acts 1:8; 2:1-4). The answer seems to be that the latter constituted an open and public confirmation of what Jesus privately bestowed on this occasion.

Jesus' words about the forgiveness of sins did not actually give the apostles the authority to forgive sins. It rather gave them the authority to declare that those who receive Christ will be forgiven and those who reject Christ will not.

Jesus' second meeting with his disciples
(vv. 24-29)

Eight days later the disciples were again together with Thomas present. Unimpressed by his fellow disciples' talk about the resurrection, he had declared that he would not believe until he could actually put his finger into the nail wounds in Jesus' hands and the spear wound in his side (v. 25).

Thomas put a condition on his faith. He demanded total evidence and affirmed that he would not be satisfied with anything less. He already had sufficient evidence for believing that Jesus had risen from the dead. He had heard the predictions of Jesus to that effect (Matt. 16:21; 20:17-19). He had seen Jesus raise three people from the dead (Mark 5:36-43; Luke 7:11-15; John 11:38-44). And he had heard the testimony of ten men whom he knew to be utterly trustworthy. Yet even with all this evidence, Thomas adamantly refused to believe.

Jesus suddenly appeared and invited Thomas to do what he said he would do (vv. 26-27). Thomas did not live up to his bold words. The fact that Jesus quoted those words precisely could mean only one thing: Jesus knew that he, Thomas, had spoken them. How could Jesus have known what he said if he were not the risen Lord? So Thomas fell at the feet of Jesus and cried: 'My Lord and my God!'

Leon Morris writes:

'In the moment that he came to see that Jesus was indeed risen from the dead Thomas came to see something of what that implied. Mere men do not rise from the dead in this fashion. The One who was now so obviously alive, though He had died, could be addressed in the language of adoring worship'

(*The Gospel According to John*, p.854).

331

Jesus responded to Thomas' confession by rebuking him over his refusal to believe in spite of sufficient evidence (v. 29). Jesus did not ask him to take a leap of faith or to straddle an impossible credibility gap but to trust on the basis of inescapable reason.

The purpose of John's Gospel (vv. 30-31)

The fact is that John wrote this Gospel to encourage his readers to say the very same thing about Jesus that Thomas said in his confession. The words 'that you may believe' should be translated 'that you may go on believing'. John certainly wanted unbelieving readers to come to faith in Christ, but he also wanted believing readers to continue in the faith. To that end, he presented only a few of the miracles Jesus performed.

If the few miracles that John presented in this Gospel are not sufficient for us to come to and to continue in the truth about Jesus, no amount of miracles will convince us.

Digging   Deeper

1. Read verses 19-20. How did Jesus convince his disciples that he had risen? What was the response of the disciples?

2. Read verses 21-23. What work did Jesus assign the disciples? What provision did he make for them?

3. *Read verses 24-25. How did Thomas respond to the report of Jesus' resurrection?*

4. *Read verses 26-29. What did Jesus ask Thomas to do? How did Thomas respond? What rebuke did Jesus offer?*

5. *Read verses 30-31. What was John's purpose in writing this Gospel?*

Thomas' sparkling confession of faith in verse 28 is one of several such confessions in the Bible. Write in the blanks provided the names that belong with the confessions:

Joshua 24:15   _____

Ruth 1:16   _____

2 Kings 5:15   _____

Matthew 16:16   _____

2 Timothy 1:12   _____

Reassurance for seven disciples

'And he said to them, "Cast the net on the right side of the boat, and you will find some." So they cast, and now they were not able to draw it in because of the multitude of fish' (v. 6).

Seven of Jesus' disciples decided to go fishing. This has sparked considerable debate among commentators. Some think these men were turning their backs on their calling to discipleship and were returning to their former livelihood. It would not be surprising if this were the case. These men had reason to believe that Jesus would want nothing more to do with them. They probably believed that they had hopelessly compromised their standing as disciples by failing to stay with Jesus when he was arrested and crucified.

Other commentators insist that there was nothing wrong in these men going fishing. They point out that these men had been riding an emotional roller coaster for several days and were now seeking some refreshment and relaxation while awaiting further orders from Jesus. These commentators commend the disciples for occupying their time with meaningful labour instead of sitting in idleness.

A context of failure

The names of the disciples

While we cannot know all that was going on in the minds of these men, it surely is not without significance that John identifies these seven disciples as he does. Of the five whom he names, Simon Peter, the denier, and Thomas, the doubter, are mentioned first. This may be John's way of establishing the context of the disciples' failures for what Jesus was about to do. While all the disciples had failed, none had failed quite so completely and dramatically as these two men.

Then John singles out for mention Nathaniel and the sons of Zebedee (John himself and his brother James). This could be his way of taking us back to the first chapter of his Gospel in which he reports how he, his brother and Nathaniel — and, yes, Simon Peter — came to follow Jesus.

The five named disciples would seem to suggest, then, that failure in discipleship did not mean the end of discipleship.

The fishing of the disciples (v. 3)

The futility of the disciples in their fishing may very well have been intended by Jesus to remind them of a previous fishing failure, which ended with them forsaking all to follow Jesus (Luke 5:1-11).

> 'The fact that the disciples caught no fish that night was no accident: it was planned in order to give these men an object lesson.
>
> 'Our Lord wanted to teach them that life outside his will is utterly futile. He graciously, firmly showed his security-seeking followers that the very best skill, exercised in the most familiar of circumstances, is no guarantee of success, outside his will. The fishing failure was love's way of showing

that there are as many perils in withdrawing from the Lord as
there may be in going on with him'

(Glyn Owen, *From Simon to Peter*, p.239).

The reassuring Saviour (vv. 4-13)

The assurance provided by the multitude of fish (vv. 4-8)

As on the occasion of their first fishing failure, Jesus arrived
on the scene and instructed them regarding their fishing.
Once again they complied with Jesus' instruction and met
with huge success (Luke 5:1-11). The fish, like the disciples
themselves, were in the hands of the sovereign Lord.

Once the disciples realized that the stranger on the shore
was Jesus (v. 7), they undoubtedly called to mind the events
described in Luke 5. And we can also be sure that they were
quick to reason that if Jesus wanted them to follow him when
he first helped them with their fishing, he must have helped
them on this occasion because he wants them to continue
following him. The Lord's calling had not been negated by
their failure.

At the same moment as they realized that Jesus still had
work for them to do, another realization must have flooded
in upon them — that the same Lord who was sufficient
for them as they cast their nets for fish would prove to be
sufficient for them in the work of fishing for men. They must
have understood that they could not possibly succeed on
their own but must depend totally upon his strength.

The assurance provided by the breakfast (vv. 9-13)

It would not be surprising if these seven disciples found
Jesus' invitation to breakfast to be even more reassuring
than the catch of fish. In that culture, an invitation to eat

involved far more than eating. It was also, even as it is today, an invitation to fellowship and communion. The very Lord whom they had failed still desired to enjoy fellowship with them!

This passage begins with the disciples on the sea and the Lord Jesus on the shore. The disciples make their way to shore in different ways and once there find food prepared and enter into communion with Jesus.

We are even now on the sea of life. It is often a turbulent sea, and we are tossed about. But our Christ stands on the heavenly shore, overseeing our labours and assuring us that his strength is sufficient for us.

One day we will ourselves make it to heaven's shore, where he will personally receive us. And there we will find a banquet spread before us such as we have never seen. Most of all, thank God, we shall engage in sweet communion with Christ — communion that will never be broken or destroyed.

The assurance provided by the appearance (v. 14)

Another assurance runs like a golden thread through those we have already noticed. The appearance of Jesus to these men constituted yet another assurance that he had risen from the dead. The apostle John closes his account of Jesus' dealings with these seven disciples by noting that this was the third time Jesus had showed himself to his disciples. The resurrection was such an incredible and phenomenal thing that more than one evidence was needed to substantiate it. Jesus graciously provided his disciples with several.

The resurrection of Jesus is vital for faith, but that certainly does not mean that faith is in jeopardy. The evidence for the resurrection is so overwhelming that faith's footing is sure.

'Jesus Christ still pursues his wayward, fearful, half-believing disciples today. He still prepares a meal for them and demonstrates his love. He still shows that nothing can frustrate him: when it is his will to give the victory, he can and does give it. Meantime, despite his disciples' failures, he only asks for brokenness, penitence and a turning afresh to love him in faith. Then they will know the flood of grace and love that his sustenance provides; then they will know as well the joy of being recommissioned... '

(Owen, pp.244-45).

DIGGING   DEEPER

1. *Read verses 1-3. What details do these verses provide about the disciples of Jesus?*

2. *Read verses 4-8. What did the stranger on the shore command? What happened? How did Simon Peter respond?*

3. *Read verses 9-14. What were Jesus' reasons for meeting and feeding these disciples?*

Draw a line from each Scripture to the individual or group to whom the risen Christ appeared:

Week 51	Foundations for the faith
Mark 16:9; John 20:11-18	the disciples without Thomas
Matthew 28:9-10	Paul
Luke 24:13-35	Mary Magdalene
Luke 24:34; 1 Corinthians 15:15	the disciples with Thomas
John 20:19-23	2 disciples journeying to Emmaus
John 20:24-29	500 disciples
1 Corinthians 15:6	Simon Peter
Acts 9:3-7	the women

Simon Peter in the grip of grace

'Jesus said to him, "If I will that he remain till I come, what is that to you? You follow me"' (v. 22).

Simon Peter had failed in a most shocking and grievous manner. On the night before Jesus was crucified, Peter denied both his faith in him and even any association with him. Simon denied even though he swore he would not. He denied with great emphasis and vehemence, even resorting to profanity in the process. He denied, not once or twice, but three times.

The passage before us presents incredibly good news for all those saints of God who have trodden or are treading the path of denial that Simon Peter walked: the Lord Jesus Christ will never let his people go.

Here we find him pursuing Simon and restoring him to fellowship with himself and to usefulness in his kingdom. Thank God for pursuing and restoring grace!

The Lord restores Simon Peter (vv. 15-17)

The restoration of Peter was worked out against a backdrop specifically designed to remind him of the denials. These had occurred as Peter warmed himself by the fire (John 18:17-18,25-27), and here he finds himself face to face with Jesus beside a fire (v. 9). Three times Peter had denied the Lord, and here he is asked three times if he truly loves the Lord.

We should also note that Jesus addressed him as 'Simon' instead of 'Peter', which means 'rock'. Peter had failed to live up to his name.

The first question included the phrase 'more than these' and is probably a reference to the other disciples. It reminded Simon Peter of his boast that he would not forsake Jesus even if all the others did (Mark 14:29).

The second and third questions exclude the comparison and simply ask Simon Peter if he could honestly affirm his love for Christ. Some have made a great deal of the fact that he and Jesus used different words for love; and other interpreters point out that the two Greek verbs for love are often used interchangeably in classical Greek literature.

The way that Jesus deals with Simon Peter in these verses ought to encourage us. No matter how his people fail, the Lord is willing to forgive and restore.

'There can be little doubt but that the whole scene is meant to show us Peter as completely restored to his position of leadership. He has three times denied his Lord. Now he has three times affirmed his love for Him, and three times he has been commissioned to care for the flock. This must have had the effect on the others of a demonstration that, whatever had been the mistakes of the past, Jesus was restoring Peter to a place of trust'

(Morris, *John*, p.875).

The Lord demands sacrificial service from Simon Peter (vv. 15-19)

It is never enough simply to profess love for Christ. True love will always reveal itself in action. Therefore, after each of Peter's affirmations of love the Lord said, 'Feed my lambs,' or 'Feed my sheep.'

Some think Jesus had in mind different age groups within the church and was calling Simon Peter to manifest his love towards the Lord by caring for the Lord's people whether they be young believers (lambs) or mature believers (sheep). Others think Jesus was looking at his people from different angles: while they are like weak lambs and straying sheep, they are always the objects of his affection.

This much is plain: there is a distinct and definite connection between loving Christ and loving his people. Commitment to Christ always involves commitment to his church. If we do not have the latter, we have no right to conclude we have the former.

'It is as if the Master says to Peter: "Simon, you were weak like a lamb, wandering like a sheep, yet, throughout it all, you, like a dear ... sheep, were the object of my tender and loving solicitude. Now, having profited by your experiences ... consider the members of my Church to be your lambs, and feed them; your sheep, and shepherd them; yes, your *dear* sheep, and in feeding them love them! *Do not neglect the work among the flock, Simon. That is your real assignment! Go back to it!"'*

(William Hendriksen, vol. ii, p.489, italics are his).

Love to Christ not only manifests itself in terms of sacrificial service but also in suffering. For Peter this would mean eventual martyrdom. God does not call all his people to die for Christ, but he does call them to suffer for him (Phil. 1:29; 2 Tim. 3:12).

> 'When we die patiently, submitting to the will of God — die cheerfully, rejoicing in hope of the glory of God — and die usefully, witnessing to the truth and goodness of religion and encouraging others, we glorify God in dying...'
>
> (Matthew Henry, vol. v, p.1233).

The Lord provides focus for Simon Peter (vv. 20-25)

When Simon Peter heard what lay ahead for him, he turned to Jesus and said, 'What about this man?' (v. 21). The Lord's revelation of martyrdom for Simon made him wonder if his dear friend John would share that fate. But, as Jesus made plain in his answer, the matter was none of Simon's business (v. 22).

This reminds us of how very easy it is for us to concern ourselves with matters that the Lord has not chosen to reveal rather than with those things that he has.

> 'There is work to be done. There are souls to be reached. There is a task to be accomplished. Let Peter rivet all his attention upon this! Some people are always asking questions. They are asking so many questions that their real mission in life fails to receive the proper amount of interest and energy'
>
> (William Hendriksen, vol. ii, p.491).

> 'Of course Jesus did not intend to suggest that we are not to take a deep interest in the fate of others, but he wishes us to be kept from all envy and discontent which comparisons may

produce; and he desires us to be concerned, rather, as to our
absolute fidelity to him'

(Charles R. Erdman, p.177).

DIGGING   DEEPER

1. *Read verses 15-19. What did Jesus ask Simon Peter? Why
   did he repeat the question three times? What prediction did
   Jesus make regarding him?*

2. *Read verses 20-23. How did Simon Peter respond to Jesus'
   prediction? How did Jesus respond to Simon's response?*

3. *Read verses 24-25. How does John identify himself here?
   What does he affirm about the Gospel he has written?*

Write beside each Scripture a short statement
about how Simon Peter was used of God after
Jesus restored him.

Acts 2:14-42   _____

_____

Acts 3:1-8   _____

_____

345

Acts 9:32-43 _____

_____

Acts 10:1-48 _____

_____

Acts 11:1-18 _____

_____

1 Peter 1:1; 2 Peter 1:1_____

_____

Bibliography

Books quoted

William Barclay, *The Gospel of John* (vol. i), The Westminster Press (Philadelphia).

James Montgomery Boice, *The Gospel of John* (five volumes in one), Zondervan Publishing House, 1985.

John Brown, *Discourses and Sayings of our Lord* (vol. iii), The Banner of Truth Trust.

John Calvin, *Calvin's Commentaries* (vols xvii, xviii), Baker Book House, 1979.

S. G. DeGraaf, *Promise and Deliverance* (vols iii and iv), Presbyterian and Reformed Publishing Co., 1979.

Charles R. Erdman, *An Exposition: The Gospel of John*, The Westminster Press, 1944.

John Gill, *Exposition of the Old and New Testaments* (vol. viii), The Baptist Standard Bearer, Inc., 1989.

William Hendriksen, *New Testament Commentary: Exposition of the Gospel According to John* (two volumes in one), Baker Book House, 1970.

Matthew Henry, *Matthew Henry's Commentary on the Whole Bible* (vol. v), Fleming H. Revell Company, no date.

Gordon J. Keddie, *A Study Commentary on John* (vols 1 and 2), Evangelical Press, 2001.

Bruce Milne, *The Bible Speaks Today: The Message of John*, Inter-Varsity Press, 1993.

Leon Morris, *The New International Commentary: The Gospel According to John*, Wm B. Eerdmans Publishing Co., 1971.

Arthur W. Pink, *Exposition of the Gospel of John* (three volumes in one), Zondervan Publishing House, 1971.

J. C. Ryle, *Expository Thoughts on John* (three volumes), The Banner of Truth Trust, 1987.

R. V. G. Tasker, *Tyndale New Testament Commentaries: The Gospel According to St John*, Wm B. Eerdmans Publishing Co., 1972.

Warren W. Wiersbe, *The Bible Exposition Commentary* (vol. i), Victor Books, 1989.

Other helpful studies

D. A. Carson, *The Gospel According to John*, Wm B. Eerdmans, 1991.

George Hutcheson, *The Gospel of John*, The Banner of Truth Trust, 1972.

Mark Johnston, *Let's Study John*, The Banner of Truth Trust, 2003.

R. C. H. Lenski, *The Interpretation of St. John's Gospel*, Augsburg Publishing House, 1961.

A wide range of Christian books is available from EP Books. If you would like a free catalogue please write to us or contact us by e-mail. Alternatively, you can view the whole catalogue online at our web site:

www.epbooks.org

EP BOOKS
Faverdale North, Darlington, DL3 0PH, England

e-mail: sales@epbooks.org

EP BOOKS USA
P. O. Box 614, Carlisle, PA 17013, USA

e-mail: usa.sales@epbooks.org